THE AUSTRALIAN
Women's Weekly

MONEY SAVING MEALS

MONEY SAVING MEALS

EASY, DELICIOUS LOW-COST FAMILY FOOD

Project Editor Siobhán O'Connor
Project Designer Alison Shackleton
Editor Lucy Sienkowska
Jacket Designer Alison Donovan
Jackets Coordinator Jasmin Lennie
Production Editor David Almond
Production Controller Rebecca Parton
Managing Editor Dawn Henderson
Managing Art Editor Alison Donovan
Art Director Maxine Pedliham
Publishing Director Katie Cowan

First published in Great Britain in 2023
by Dorling Kindersley Limited
DK, One Embassy Gardens, 8 Viaduct Gardens, London, SW11 7BW

The authorized representative in the EEA is Dorling Kindersley
Verlag GmbH. Arnulfstr. 124, 80636 Munich, Germany

Copyright © 2023 Dorling Kindersley Limited
A Penguin Random House Company
10 9 8 7 6 5 4 3 2 1
001–333816–Mar/2023

A CIP catalogue record for this book is available from the British Library.
ISBN: 978-0-2415-9823-8

Printed and bound in China

For the curious
www.dk.com

This book was made with Forest Stewardship Council™ certified paper –
one small step in DK's commitment to a sustainable future.
For more information go to **www.dk.com/our-green-pledge**

Contents

Money-saving meals

Minding your money shouldn't mean sacrificing a flavoursome and filling meal. With just a few simple tricks, you can make the most out of your cooking, without breaking the bank. Here's how to stretch the household budget and go thrifty on dinner, without any compromise on satisfaction.

Meal planning

A budget-friendly meal comes down to proper prior planning. The valuable time taken to plan your meals means you'll arrive at the shops prepared and avoid any last-minute dashes to expensive corner shops or unnecessary trips to the supermarket where you will be tempted to pop extra items in the basket.

Select from a variety of hearty and fresh meals to bring variety to your week, considering dishes that can provide multiple days' worth of food. You could take any remaining Sherry Braised Beef (page 76), for example, and revitalize it the following day with mash (page 26) and garlicky beans (page 106).

When planning, always bring your menus back to what you already have in the pantry. Consider any lingering and long-lasting legumes, pulses, or grains you have, and use these to build your meals. Utilize any canned beans and transform them into a fresh take on baked beans served alongside cheesy squash (page 141), for instance, for a hearty meat-free meal.

As you develop your meal plan, be sure to make use of what is in season, as this will ensure both a strong availability of these ingredients and being able to buy them at a more reasonable price. Produce that has been grown and harvested during its peak growth period is abundant, cheaper, and fresher – and tastes better, too.

Shopping

If you make certain of one thing, let it be writing a considered shopping list. This will be your best guide to keeping on track at the supermarket. You can use the list to direct and merge buying for meals where ingredients are often bought cheaper in bulk or whole. Take a whole bunch of celery and use some of it for the chunky minestrone on page 10, then use the remainder for apricot chicken (page 101). Also, perishables such as olive oil that have a longer shelf life are more economical if you buy in quantity, rather than in small amounts. But buy only what you know you will be able to use before they spoil.

For ultimate ease, categorize your items by the way they are found at the supermarket or shopping centre. As well as keeping your trip efficient as you work your way through the aisles and sections, this will highlight any potentially available substitutes you may already have on hand at home. If there is an opened bottle of vinegar in your cupboard, consider changing the style suggested in the recipe and using what you have instead; similarly, don't be wedded to a recipe's serving suggestion, if one type of rice is called for and you have another, use that to avoid multiple half-used opened packets.

Just as you can make basic ingredient swaps according to your pantry, you can apply the same flexibility at the shops. If a wedge of Parmesan is pushing the pounds up, you can still get your cheesy hit by choosing a more affordable option such as Cheddar. Bear in mind, too, that a little Parmesan usually goes a long way, so you will not need to use as much as other, less flavourful cheeses – which is its own built-in economy. If using two herbs turns out to be quite expensive, pick your preferred one and go from there. Let availability and cost be your guide.

Bulk cooking

Give your future self a leg up for the week with a helpful batch of bulk cooking. This is an ideal way to bring multiple lives to a meal and prevent any avoidable food waste. Incorporate this into your weekly meal planning to provide a busy weeknight saviour in minutes. Be sure to thank yourself later.

Either directly set aside and store any remaining portions of your dish or use these leftovers as a springboard for your next meal. Take any larger cuts of meat, such as the red-cooked pork on page 70, and pair a second or third time with an alternative grain, fresh zingy salad, or tossed through noodles.

Make the most of your freezer, too. Stock up on reusable containers or seal your meals in resealable plastic bags to freeze lying flat to be extra space-savvy. Before filling with food, always date and label the containers or bags to ensure you use the oldest first and don't end up with an unexpected stew or waste food by not using it in time. A stored protein or meal is just the thing for filling a void in your meal plan down the road—and you've already paid for it.

Storage

An obvious way to get the most life out of your ingredients is to store them correctly. Lengthen their shelf life with a few easy tricks that will allow you to carry on using them long after purchasing.

For herbs, store in a jar of water in or out of the fridge, or wrap in a slightly damp clean cloth and store sealed in the fridge. Treat leafy greens and vegetables much the same, avoiding the plastic packaging often found in the supermarkets. Ensure mushrooms are stored in a paper bag in the fridge to avoid a build-up of moisture.

Some ingredients are best stored at ambient temperature. Keep dry foods such as rice and dried pasta in plastic, glass, or metal containers to guard against pantry predators. Store earthy vegetables such as onions, potatoes, and whole squash in a cool, dark, dry place. To allow them to ripen properly and develop their natural sweetness, keep fresh fruit – including tomatoes – out on the worktop.

SOUPS, CURRIES, AND CASSEROLES

Simple to make and richly flavoured, from hearty stews and chill-busting soups to meltingly tender slow-cooked classics, these meals are like being hugged from the inside.

Chunky minestrone with Halloumi

DOUBLE BATCH | PREP + COOK TIME **1 HOUR 30 MINUTES + OVERNIGHT STANDING** | SERVES **8**

Hearty and nutritious, this soup is ideal for making up and chilling or freezing half to have on hand for another day. The vegetables and type of dried beans used in the recipe are entirely flexible – just swap them, weight for weight, according to the season and price.

You will need to start this recipe a day ahead

$^2/_3$ cup (130g) dried red kidney beans

$^1/_3$ cup (65g) raw buckwheat or buckinis (see tips)

$^1/_4$ cup (60ml) olive oil

1 leek (350g), white part only, thinly sliced

200g smoked streaky bacon, coarsely chopped

1 large carrot (180g), coarsely chopped

2 trimmed celery sticks (200g), coarsely chopped

2 parsnips (500g), finely chopped

1 orange sweet potato (400g), coarsely chopped

2 large courgettes (300g), diced

2 x 400g cans diced tomatoes

3 vegetable stock cubes (30g), crumbled

1 dried bay leaf

salt and freshly ground black pepper

250g Halloumi cheese, thickly sliced (see tips)

$^1/_2$ cup (125ml) pesto

TIPS

- Buckinis, also known as activated buckwheat groats, are nutritionally dense and great in soups.
- Stock cubes are handy alternatives to liquid stock and easy to keep in your pantry. You can also use the equivalent of a concentrated stock base from a jar.
- The Halloumi is enough for 4 portions of soup. Cook up some more when you reheat the leftovers.
- You can refrigerate the minestrone for up to 3 days. Alternatively, freeze for up to 3 months; thaw in the fridge, then reheat in a microwave.

1 The day before cooking the minestrone, put the kidney beans and buckwheat in separate medium bowls with enough cold water in each to cover. Allow to stand overnight, before draining the kidney beans and buckwheat separately; rinse under cold water.

2 Put the kidney beans in a saucepan of boiling water; return to the boil. Boil for 10 minutes. Reduce the heat to medium; simmer for 10 minutes or until the beans are just tender. Drain. Set aside until needed.

3 Heat half of the olive oil in a large heavy-based saucepan over a medium heat; cook the leek and bacon, stirring, for 10 minutes or until the leek is softened. Add the carrot and celery; cook, stirring, for 5 minutes. Add the parsnips, sweet potato, courgettes, diced tomatoes, crumbled stock cubes, 1.85 litres water, and bay leaf; bring to the boil. Reduce the heat to low; cook, covered, for 30 minutes.

4 Stir in the buckwheat; cook, covered, for a further 15 minutes or until the buckwheat is tender. Remove the lid, and add the kidney beans to the soup; cook, uncovered, for a further 5 minutes or until warmed through. Season with salt and pepper to taste.

5 Heat the remaining olive oil in a medium frying pan over a medium heat; cook the Halloumi, in batches, until browned on both sides.

6 Serve half of the minestrone topped with the Halloumi (see tips) and a drizzle of pesto. Transfer the remaining minestrone to an airtight container; allow to cool, then store until needed (see tips).

Richest beef casserole

DOUBLE BATCH | PREP + COOK TIME **2 HOURS 45 MINUTES** | SERVES **8**

One of the more economical cuts of beef, feather blade is cut from the shoulder. Full of flavour, it really benefits from long, slow braising and roasting. You don't need to use an expensive wine, just a good-quality one you would happily drink, or use beer or cider instead.

1.7kg piece of beef feather blade roast, excess fat trimmed

1/4 cup (40g) plain flour

1/4 cup (60ml) olive oil

8 shallots, peeled, with root ends intact

2 carrots (240g), thickly sliced

1 trimmed celery stick (100g), thickly sliced

4 garlic cloves, crushed

2 tbsp thyme leaves, plus extra, to serve

2 tbsp tomato purée

1 cup (250ml) red wine or beer or cider

2 tbsp red wine or balsamic vinegar

2 beef stock cubes (20g), crumbled

60g dark chocolate (70% cocoa), finely chopped

salt and freshly ground black pepper

1 Preheat the oven to 180°C (160°C fan/350°F/Gas 4).

2 Cut the beef into 4cm pieces. Put the beef and flour in a large bowl; season with salt and pepper to taste. Toss to coat the beef evenly in the flour, shaking off any excess flour.

3 Heat 1 tablespoon of the olive oil in a 5-litre cast-iron or other heavy-based flameproof casserole over a high heat. Cook half of the beef, turning, for 5 minutes or until well browned. Transfer the beef to a large bowl. Repeat with another 1 tablespoon of the olive oil and the remaining beef; transfer to the same bowl.

4 Reduce the heat to medium; add the remaining olive oil, shallots, carrots, celery, garlic, and the 2 tablespoons thyme. Cook, stirring, for 2 minutes or until the garlic is fragrant. Add the tomato purée; cook, stirring, for 3 minutes or until the mixture looks almost dry. Add the wine, scraping the bottom of the pan with the spoon to deglaze. Bring to the boil; simmer for 2 minutes.

5 Return the beef to the casserole; stir in the vinegar, crumbled stock cubes, and 1 litre water. Cover the surface of the casserole with a large piece of baking parchment, ensuring the mixture is completely covered; cover with a tight-fitting lid. Transfer the dish to the oven; bake, stirring occasionally, for 1 1/2 hours. Remove the lid and baking parchment; cook for a further 30 minutes or until the beef is tender. Stir in the chocolate until melted.

6 Serve half of the beef casserole topped with extra thyme. Transfer the remaining beef casserole to an airtight container; allow to cool, then store until needed (see tips).

TIPS

• Serve with Garlicky Beans with Pine Nuts (page 106) and creamy mashed potato (page 26).

• You can refrigerate the beef casserole for up to 3 days. Alternatively, freeze for up to 3 months; thaw in the fridge, then reheat in a microwave.

Spinach and paneer curry

VEGETARIAN | PREP + COOK TIME **35 MINUTES** | SERVES **4**

Paneer is a good protein and calcium option for those on a vegetarian diet, while spinach is rich in calcium, potassium, and folate. This no-waste recipe, echoing the Indian classic sag paneer, uses all of the coriander bunch – leaves, stems, and roots, if they are attached.

$^3/_4$ cup (150g) brown rice

4 tsp olive oil

1 onion (150g), thinly sliced

1 tbsp ginger paste

2 garlic cloves, crushed

1 bunch of coriander (100g), leaves separated, roots and stems washed, coarsely chopped

1 long green chilli, thinly sliced

120g baby spinach leaves

200g paneer cheese, cut into 2cm cubes

1 tbsp garam masala

2 tsp ground cumin

400g canned chickpeas, drained, rinsed

$^1/_3$ cup (95g) plain yogurt

salt and freshly ground black pepper

1 small lemon, cut into wedges, to serve

1 Cook the rice according to the packet directions. Drain; cover to keep warm.

2 Meanwhile, heat 2 teaspoons of the olive oil in a medium heavy-based frying pan over a medium-high heat. Add the onion; cook, stirring, for 5 minutes or until soft. Add the ginger, garlic, coriander stems and roots, and half of the green chilli; cook for 1 minute or until fragrant. Add the spinach; cook for 1 minute or until just wilted.

3 Transfer the spinach mixture to a food processor with the coriander leaves; pulse until coarsely chopped. Set aside until needed.

4 Heat the remaining 2 teaspoons olive oil in the same pan over a medium-high heat. Add the paneer; cook, turning, for 2 minutes. Add the garam masala and cumin; cook, stirring, for 1 minute or until fragrant.

5 Return the spinach mixture to the pan, then add the chickpeas and yogurt. Remove from the heat; stir until well combined. Season with salt and pepper to taste.

6 Divide the brown rice and paneer mixture evenly among 4 serving bowls. Sprinkle with the remaining chilli; serve with the lemon wedges for squeezing over.

TIP

Paneer (or panir) is a fresh, unripened cow's milk cheese similar to pressed ricotta. It has a crumbly texture and mild flavour, and is usually available in the chilled section of major supermarkets, as well as at some health food shops and South Asian grocers.

Spicy lamb and chickpea casserole

DOUBLE BATCH | PREP + COOK TIME **2 HOURS 40 MINUTES** | SERVES **8**

When tomatoes are expensive or out of season, substitute a 400g can chopped tomatoes in place of the fresh tomatoes. Serve the casserole with bought flatbread or any other style of bread you have on hand, for mopping up the delicious casserole sauce. And if you have fresh herbs on hand, a handful of mint or flat-leaf parsley can be added for serving.

1 tbsp olive oil

2kg lamb neck chops, excess fat trimmed (see tips)

2 onions (300g), coarsely chopped

3 garlic cloves, crushed

1 tbsp finely grated fresh root ginger

2 long red chillies, seeded, finely chopped

3 tsp ground cumin

2 tsp garam masala

2 cinnamon sticks

2 tbsp plain flour

1 litre beef stock

400g can chickpeas, drained, rinsed

3 tomatoes (480g), quartered

salt and freshly ground black pepper

fresh herbs of choice such as mint, rosemary, or flat-leaf parsley, to serve (optional)

1 Preheat the oven to 160°C (140°C fan/325°F/Gas 3).

2 Heat half of the olive oil in a 5-litre cast-iron or other flameproof casserole over a high heat. Cook the lamb in batches, turning, for 3 minutes or until browned all over; transfer each batch to a large heatproof bowl.

3 Heat the remaining olive oil in the same dish; cook the onions, stirring, for 3 minutes or until golden. Add the garlic, ginger, chillies, cumin, garam masala, and cinnamon; cook, stirring, for 30 seconds or until fragrant. Add the flour; cook, stirring, for 30 seconds. Gradually add the beef stock, stirring to combine.

4 Return the lamb to the casserole with the chickpeas; bring to the boil over a high heat. Cover with a tight-fitting lid. Transfer to the oven; cook for 1 hour. Add the tomatoes, then return to the oven; cook, stirring occasionally, for a further 1 hour or until the lamb is tender and the tomatoes soften.

5 Remove and discard the cinnamon sticks; season with salt and pepper to taste. Serve half of the lamb casserole topped with fresh herbs, if you like. Transfer the remaining lamb casserole to an airtight container; allow to cool, then store until needed (see tip).

TIPS

- Look for lamb neck chops at your local butcher or at the meat counter of larger supermarkets, or use forequarter chops instead, if you like.
- You can refrigerate the lamb casserole for up to 3 days. Alternatively, freeze for up to 3 months; thaw in the fridge, then reheat in a microwave.

Autumn chicken fricassee with buttermilk scones

DO-AHEAD | PREP + COOK TIME **1 HOUR 5 MINUTES** | SERVES **4**

This comforting stew can be prepared to the end of step 4 up to two days in advance, then refrigerated in an airtight container until you are ready. Reheat in the same dish initially used for cooking, then proceed with the recipe 30 minutes before you wish to serve.

1–2 tbsp olive oil

4 chicken thigh fillets (680g), cut into thirds

1 large onion (200g), thinly sliced

2 garlic cloves, crushed

4 portobello mushrooms (200g), thickly sliced

200g chestnut mushrooms, quartered

1/2 cup (125ml) dry white wine

2 chicken stock cubes (20g), crumbled

400g kipfler (fingerling) potatoes, unpeeled, thickly sliced on the diagonal

1 tbsp thyme leaves

2 tbsp coarsely chopped sage

salt and freshly ground black pepper

buttermilk scones

2 cups (300g) self-raising flour

1/4 tsp bicarbonate of soda

1 tsp sea salt flakes

60g cold butter, coarsely chopped

3/4 cup (180ml) buttermilk or plain yogurt or milk

1 tbsp thyme leaves, plus extra 2 tsp finely chopped

1 tbsp finely chopped sage leaves

olive oil cooking spray

1 Heat the olive oil in a cast-iron or similar flameproof casserole over a high heat. Add the chicken; cook for 3 minutes on each side or until golden and caramelized. Transfer to a plate.

2 Reduce the heat to medium, add the onion; cook, stirring, for 5 minutes or until softened. Add the garlic and all the mushrooms; cook, stirring, for 8 minutes or until the mushrooms are softened. Add the wine, bring to a simmer; cook for 5 minutes or until reduced slightly.

3 Return the chicken to the pan. Add the stock cubes, 3 cups (750ml) water, and potatoes; bring to the boil; reduce the heat to low-medium. Cook, covered, for 25 minutes. Remove the lid; cook for a further 10 minutes or until the chicken and potatoes are tender and the sauce reduces slightly.

4 Meanwhile, to make the buttermilk scones, preheat the oven to 180°C (160°C fan/350°F/Gas 4). Grease and line a large baking tray with baking parchment. Put the flour, bicarbonate of soda, and salt in a medium bowl; rub in the butter using your fingertips. Stir in the buttermilk, the 1 tablespoon thyme leaves, and sage to make a soft, sticky dough. Place 12 separate spoonfuls of the dough onto the lined tray; spray lightly with the olive oil cooking spray. Bake for 15 minutes or until light golden and cooked through. Transfer the scones to a wire rack to cool.

5 Sprinkle the chicken fricassee with the thyme and sage; season with salt and pepper to taste. Serve with the buttermilk scones.

TIP

To make a one-pot dish, drop spoonfuls of the dough directly onto the stew; cook, covered, for 10 minutes, then uncovered for a further 8 minutes or until the dumplings spring back when lightly pressed.

Thai green pork curry

VEGETABLE SWAP | PREP + COOK TIME **35 MINUTES** | SERVES **4**

This fragrant curry with its creamy sauce is a great opportunity to use up any vegetables you might have on hand in the vegetable crisper, in place of the green beans. You could also try chopped leafy greens, cauliflower, or broccoli florets. And it couldn't be simpler to put together, easily outstripping offerings from your local takeaway in zest and freshness.

800g pork mince

3 tsp ginger paste (see tips)

1 long red chilli, finely chopped (see tips)

2 garlic cloves, crushed

$^1/_3$ cup coarsely chopped coriander

1 tbsp groundnut oil or other oil of your choice

$^1/_4$ cup (75g) Thai green curry paste

2 x 400ml cans coconut milk

$^2/_3$ cup (130g) jasmine rice

2 tbsp lime juice

1 tbsp fish sauce

1 tbsp grated palm sugar

200g green beans, trimmed

$^1/_3$ cup Thai basil or basil leaves

lime cheeks, to serve (optional)

1 Combine the pork, ginger paste, chilli, garlic, and half of the coriander in a medium bowl; roll level tablespoons of the mixture into balls. Heat the groundnut oil in a large frying pan over a high heat; cook the meatballs, in batches, for 5 minutes or until browned all over. Remove from the pan.

2 Cook the green curry paste in the same pan over a medium heat, stirring, for 30 seconds or until fragrant. Add the coconut milk; bring to the boil. Reduce the heat; simmer, stirring occasionally, for about 10 minutes.

3 Meanwhile, boil, steam, or microwave the jasmine rice according to the packet directions until tender.

4 Return the meatballs to the pan with the lime juice, fish sauce, palm sugar, and beans; simmer, covered, for 5 minutes or until the meatballs are cooked through. Remove from the heat; stir in the basil and the remaining coriander. Serve the curry with the jasmine rice and lime cheeks for squeezing over, if you like.

TIPS

▪ Ginger paste is a great pantry staple to have on hand when you don't want to purchase fresh ginger. Choose a quality brand and watch out for additives.

▪ The fresh chilli can be replaced with 1 teaspoon chilli paste, $^1/_2$ teaspoon chilli flakes, or $^1/_4$ teaspoon chilli powder, if you like.

Bacon, potato, and chicken chowder

DO-AHEAD | PREP + COOK TIME **40 MINUTES** | SERVES **4**

Often based on milk or cream, chowder is usually thickened with a roux or crumbled crackers, and makes for a satisfying meal in a bowl. To extend this comforting version, add a drained large (400g) can of sweetcorn kernels or 1 cup (150g) frozen sweetcorn to the soup with the chicken, if you like, and serve with hot, buttered toast or fresh, crusty bread.

250g streaky bacon rashers, coarsely chopped

6 spring onions, coarsely chopped

2 garlic cloves, crushed

40g butter

$1/3$ cup (50g) plain flour

3 cups (750ml) milk

2 chicken stock cubes (20g)

3 cups (750ml) boiling water

3 potatoes (600g), peeled, cut into 1.5cm cubes

480g roast skinless boneless cooked chicken breasts, shredded

salt and freshly ground black pepper

1 Cook the bacon, stirring, in a large saucepan over a medium heat, for 5 minutes or until browned.

2 Add the white parts of the spring onions and the garlic to the pan; cook, stirring, for 3 minutes or until the onion is soft. Remove the bacon mixture from the saucepan.

3 Melt the butter in the same saucepan over a medium heat. Add the flour; cook, stirring, until the mixture becomes a smooth paste. Pour the milk in slowly, a little bit at a time, stirring until the mixture is smooth before adding more milk. Stir in the stock cubes and boiling water; cook, stirring, until the mixture boils and thickens.

4 Add the potatoes; simmer, covered, for about 10 minutes, stirring occasionally, until the potatoes are soft. Return the bacon mixture to the pan with the chicken; simmer, uncovered, for 2 minutes or until the chicken is hot. Season with salt and pepper to taste.

5 Serve the soup sprinkled with the remaining spring onion.

TIP

The soup can be made a day ahead; refrigerate, covered, in an airtight container until needed. It will thicken on refrigeration, so you may need a little extra milk or water to thin it. Gently reheat.

Pork and cider stew with mushrooms

DOUBLE BATCH | PREP + COOK TIME **2 HOURS 15 MINUTES** | SERVES **8**

Hot, thick, and hearty, this glorious slow-cooked stew is the ultimate comfort food for a cool autumn or winter's evening. Serve with mashed potato (see page 26) mixed through with a handful of shredded kale, or on a bed of noodles such as fettucine or pappardelle.

2kg boneless pork shoulder, excess fat trimmed, cut into 4cm pieces (see tips)

$1/3$ cup (50g) plain flour

$1/4$ cup (60ml) olive oil

8 shallots, thinly sliced

3 garlic cloves, thinly sliced

400g small chestnut mushrooms, trimmed

$1^1/2$ tbsp coarsely chopped rosemary

$1^1/2$ cups (375ml) apple cider (see tips)

2 chicken stock cubes (20g), crumbled

2 tbsp tomato purée

salt and freshly ground black pepper

1 Toss the pork in flour seasoned with salt and pepper; shake off any excess. Heat the olive oil in a 7-litre cast-iron or other flameproof casserole or a large heavy-based saucepan. Cook the pork, in batches, for 5 minutes or until browned; transfer each batch to a large heatproof bowl. Set aside to keep warm.

2 Add the shallots to the same dish with the garlic, mushrooms, and rosemary; cook, stirring occasionally, for 5 minutes or until the mushrooms are browned. Add the apple cider; cook, stirring, for 30 seconds.

3 Return the pork to the casserole with the stock cubes, 1 litre water, and the tomato purée; bring to the boil. Reduce the heat to low; cook, covered, stirring occasionally, for $1^3/4$ hours or until the pork is tender. Season with salt and pepper to taste.

4 Serve half of the pork stew. Transfer the remaining stew to an airtight container; allow to cool, then store until needed (see tips).

TIPS

▪ We trimmed and cut the pork, but you can use ready-diced pork shoulder instead for convenience.

▪ If you like, use Marsala, an Italian fortified wine with an intense amber colour and complex aroma, instead of cider; you could also substitute the cider with Madeira, port, or dry sherry.

▪ Refrigerate the pork stew for up to 3 days. Alternatively, freeze for up to 3 months; thaw in the fridge, then reheat in a microwave.

Grains and mash

Skip the plain white rice or fresh, crusty bread, and instead make one of these tasty sides to accompany a rich stew or spicy curry. With these mashes and grain salads perfect for sopping up any oozy extra juices, you won't let a single drop of sauce go to waste.

Mashed potato

PREP + COOK TIME **30 MINUTES** | SERVES **4**

Put 1kg coarsely chopped peeled potatoes in a medium saucepan with enough cold water to barely cover the potatoes. Boil over a medium heat for 15 minutes or until the potatoes are tender; drain. Using the back of a wooden spoon, push the potatoes through a fine sieve into a large bowl. Stir 40g butter and ³/4 cup (185ml) hot milk into the potato, folding gently until the mash is smooth and fluffy. Season with salt and freshly ground black pepper to taste.

Pine nut and parsley quinoa

PREP + COOK TIME **20 MINUTES** | SERVES **4**

Put 1 cup (200g) quinoa and 2 cups (500ml) water in a medium saucepan; bring to the boil. Reduce the heat to low; cook, covered, for 12 minutes or until the water is absorbed and the quinoa is tender. Stir in ¹/3 cup (50g) toasted pine nuts, 2 teaspoons finely grated lemon zest, 2 tablespoons lemon juice, and ¹/2 cup finely chopped flat-leaf parsley; season with salt and freshly ground black pepper to taste.

Lemon pistachio couscous

PREP + COOK TIME **15 MINUTES** | SERVES **4**

Combine 1 cup (190g) couscous, ³/4 cup (185ml) boiling water, 2 teaspoons finely grated lemon zest, and ¹/4 cup lemon juice in a medium heatproof bowl. Cover; allow to stand for 5 minutes or until the liquid is absorbed, fluffing with a fork occasionally. Meanwhile, cook ¹/2 cup (75g) shelled pistachios in a heated small dry frying pan until fragrant; coarsely chop. Heat 2 teaspoons olive oil in the same pan. Add 1 crushed garlic clove and 1 finely chopped small red onion; cook, stirring, until the onion softens. Fluff the couscous, then stir the pistachios, onion mixture, and ¹/2 cup (25g) shredded mint leaves through the couscous.

Soft polenta

PREP + COOK TIME **20 MINUTES** | SERVES **6**

Combine 3 cups (750ml) milk and 2 cups (500ml) chicken stock in a large saucepan; bring to the boil. Gradually add 2 cups (380g) polenta to the liquid, stirring constantly. Reduce the heat; simmer, stirring, for 10 minutes or until the polenta thickens. Add 1 cup (250ml) milk and ¹/4 cup (25g) finely grated Parmesan; stir until the Parmesan melts. Season with salt and freshly ground black pepper to taste; top with extra grated Parmesan, if you like.

Chicken and leek stew

DOUBLE BATCH | PREP + COOK TIME **1 HOUR 50 MINUTES** | SERVES **8**

Leeks are one of those overlooked and inexpensive ingredients that impart a depth and sweetness that here pairs well with the warm earthiness of mushrooms. Tarragon provides its signature anise flavour, too, but it's easily substituted with a few sprigs of thyme or rosemary.

2 small whole chickens (2.4kg)

1/3 cup (80ml) extra virgin olive oil

500g small button mushrooms

3 shallots or 1 onion (150g), thinly sliced

1 cup (250ml) grape juice or apple juice

3 large leeks (about 1kg), white part only, cut into 5cm lengths

1/4 cup (5g) tarragon leaves, chopped, plus extra 2 stems, leaves separated, to serve

2 chicken stock cubes (20g), dissolved in 2 cups (500ml) water

salt and freshly ground black pepper

1   Place one of the chickens, breast-side down, on a chopping board. Cut down both sides of the backbone using kitchen scissors; discard the backbone (or reserve for another use; see tips). Turn the chicken over; press down firmly and steadily onto the breastbone to break, so the chicken lies flat. Pat the chicken dry with kitchen paper. Repeat with the remaining chicken.

2   Heat 1 tablespoon of the olive oil in a 7-litre cast-iron or other flameproof casserole over a high heat. Add one of the chickens, breast-side down; cook, pressing the legs down so that they touch the bottom of the dish, for 10 minutes or until the chicken is golden brown. Transfer to a large plate or tray. Repeat with another tablespoon of the olive oil and the remaining chicken; transfer to a large plate or tray.

3   Add the mushrooms and shallots to the same casserole; cook, stirring, for 5 minutes or until golden brown. Add the grape juice, scraping the bottom of the dish to deglaze; cook for 1 minute or until simmering. Return the chickens to the dish, side by side. Top with the leeks and chopped tarragon, and pour over the chicken stock. Season with salt and pepper to taste. Reduce the heat to low; cook, covered with a tight-fitting lid, for 1 hour or until the chickens are cooked through.

4   Heat the remaining olive oil in a small frying pan over a low heat; cook the extra tarragon for 20 seconds or until crisp. Drain on kitchen paper.

5   Allow the stew to stand in the casserole, still covered, for 5 minutes. Transfer one of the chickens to a serving platter; cut into 4 pieces. Spoon over half of the mushrooms, leeks, and sauce, then top with the crisp-fried tarragon.

6   Cut the remaining chicken into 4 pieces; transfer to an airtight container with the remaining vegetables and sauce. Allow to cool, then store until needed (see tips).

TIPS

• Freeze the unused backbones to make your own chicken stock.

• If you like, use 1 tablespoon dried tarragon in place of the fresh, omitting the fried tarragon for serving.

• Refrigerate the stew in an airtight container for up to 2 days. Alternatively, freeze for up to 3 months; thaw in the fridge, then reheat in a microwave.

Ginger and mango chutney pork belly casserole

DOUBLE BATCH | PREP + COOK TIME **3 HOURS 10 MINUTES** | SERVES **8**

This casserole is redolent with an array of warming spices. All that's needed to round it out for a complete meal is some steamed white or brown rice. And for those of us who think crisp crackling is the best part of pork belly, that's included too!

1.8kg boneless pork belly (see tips)

1 tbsp sea salt flakes

1 tsp table salt

6 spring onions (150g), sliced

1 bunch of coriander (100g), roots chopped, leaves picked

4 garlic cloves, crushed

1 tbsp ginger paste

3 long red chillies, seeded, thinly sliced

³/₄ cup (275g) mango chutney

1 tbsp fish sauce

2³/₄ cups (680ml) vegetable stock (see tips)

salt and freshly ground black pepper

TIPS

- For best results, start the crackling a day ahead. Remove the skin from the pork; score and refrigerate overnight, covered with a tea towel, to dry out.
- You can swap the liquid stock for 2 vegetable stock cubes (20g) dissolved in 2³/₄ cups (680ml) boiling water, if you like.
- Refrigerate the pork belly casserole for up to 3 days. Alternatively, freeze for up to 3 months; thaw in the fridge, then reheat in a microwave.

1 Preheat the oven to 200°C (180°C fan/400°F/Gas 6). Line a large baking tray with baking parchment. Place a wire rack on top to fit inside the tray.

2 To remove the skin from the pork belly, run a knife horizontally between the fat and the skin. Remove as much fat from the skin as possible (this helps the crackling to become crunchy and also prevents the casserole from being too fatty). Place the skin, fat-side down, on a board; score with a sharp knife at 4mm intervals, taking care not to cut all the way through the skin. Transfer the pork skin, still fat-side down, to the prepared rack; rub the skin evenly with the sea and table salts. Cook on the top shelf of the oven for 1¹/₂ hours or until crisp and golden. Set aside at room temperature until ready to serve.

3 Reduce the oven temperature to 180°C (160°C fan/350°F/Gas 4).

4 Cut the pork belly into 4cm pieces. Heat a 7-litre cast-iron or other flameproof casserole over a high heat. Cook the pork, in batches, turning, for 6 minutes or until browned (enough fat should render out of the pork to cook with, so you won't need to add any oil); transfer each batch to a large heatproof bowl.

5 Return all of the browned pork to the casserole with the spring onions, coriander roots, garlic, ginger paste, and chilli; cook, stirring, for 2 minutes or until the spring onions soften slightly. Stir in the mango chutney, fish sauce, and vegetable stock; bring to a simmer. Cover the dish with a tight-fitting lid.

6 Transfer the dish to the oven; bake for 2 hours or until the pork is tender and almost falling apart. Season with salt and pepper to taste.

7 Serve half of the pork belly casserole with the crackling and topped with the coriander leaves. Transfer the remaining pork belly casserole to an airtight container; allow to cool, then store until needed (see tips).

Hearty pork and chorizo soup

DOUBLE BATCH | PREP + COOK TIME **2 HOURS 40 MINUTES + STANDING** | SERVES **8**

Slow-cooked so the pork is meltingly tender, this flavoursome soup is also packed with cannellini beans for a truly satisfying lunch or supper. Serve with tortilla chips for a little crunch or with crusty bread rolls for mopping up the juices.

¹/₄ cup (60ml) olive oil

1.5kg boneless shoulder of pork, excess fat trimmed, cut into 5cm pieces

1 large red onion (200g), finely chopped, reserving 1 tbsp, to serve (optional)

2 cured chorizo sausages (300g), thinly sliced

2 red peppers (350g), finely chopped

4 garlic cloves, finely chopped

2 tbsp chopped oregano leaves

1 tbsp smoked paprika

¹/₄ tsp ground cumin

2–3 tbsp chipotle chilli paste

2 ripe tomatoes (300g), seeded, finely chopped

4 chicken stock cubes (40g)

400g can cannellini beans, drained, rinsed

salt and freshly ground black pepper

coriander leaves, to serve (optional)

1   Heat the olive oil in a 6.75-litre cast-iron or other flameproof casserole or large heavy-based saucepan over a medium heat. Cook the pork in batches, stirring, for 6 minutes or until browned all over; transfer each batch to a large heatproof bowl.

2   Add the onion and chorizo to the casserole with the red peppers and garlic; cook, stirring occasionally, for 5 minutes or until softened. Add the oregano, smoked paprika, cumin, and chipotle paste; cook, stirring, for 2 minutes or until fragrant. Stir in the tomatoes.

3   Return the pork to the casserole. Dissolve the stock cubes in 1.75 litres water. Pour the stock into the casserole; bring to the boil. Reduce the heat to low; cook for 2 hours, skimming the surface occasionally to remove fat, or until the pork is very tender. Shred the meat using 2 forks, then return to the dish. Add the cannellini beans; simmer for 5 minutes or until heated through. Season with salt and pepper to taste.

4   Serve half of the soup topped with the reserved red onion and the coriander leaves, if you like. Transfer the remaining soup to an airtight container; allow to cool, then store until needed (see tips).

TIPS

- For a more pronounced chilli taste, use 3 tablespoons of the chipotle chilli paste.
- Refrigerate the soup for up to 3 days. Alternatively, freeze for up to 3 months; thaw in the fridge, then reheat in a microwave.

Slow-cooked pork neck with fennel and beans

DOUBLE BATCH | PREP + COOK TIME **2 HOURS 40 MINUTES** | SERVES **8**

Pork neck fillet is a little bit of a misnomer, as this cut derives from the shoulder of the animal. Also called boneless shoulder, this underrated cut is relatively inexpensive and its marbled meat is rendered melt-in-your-mouth tender during slow cooking.

2 tbsp fennel seeds

1 tbsp sea salt flakes

1.5kg pork neck fillet (boneless shoulder of pork), cut into 4cm pieces

2 tbsp olive oil

2 leeks (700g), white part only, thinly sliced

4 fennel bulbs (1.2kg), quartered, fronds reserved

2 cups (500ml) apple cider (see tips)

1 chicken stock cube (10g), crumbled

$1^{1}/_{2}$ cups (375ml) boiling water

400g can borlotti beans, drained, rinsed

5 wide strips of lemon zest

salt and freshly ground black pepper

mashed potato, to serve (see page 26)

1   Preheat the oven to 160°C (140°C fan/325°F/Gas 3).

2   Using a mortar and pestle, or a spice grinder, coarsely grind the fennel seeds; combine with the salt.

3   Pat the pork dry with kitchen paper. Put the pork in a bowl with the fennel salt; toss to lightly coat the pork in the salt mixture.

4   Heat 1 tablespoon of the olive oil in a 6.75-litre cast-iron or other flameproof casserole. Cook the pork in 2 batches, stirring, for 10 minutes or until browned, adding additional oil as needed; transfer each batch to a plate.

5   Heat the remaining olive oil in the same dish. Cook the leeks, stirring, for 3 minutes or until golden. Add the fennel; cook, stirring, for 5 minutes or until golden.

6   Return the pork to the dish together with the apple cider, stock cube, the $1^{1}/_{2}$ cups (375ml) boiling water, borlotti beans, and lemon zest; bring to a simmer. Cover with a tight-fitting lid. Transfer to the oven; bake, stirring occasionally, for 2 hours or until the pork is very tender. Season with salt and pepper to taste.

7   Serve half of the pork mixture topped with the reserved fennel fronds, accompanied by the mashed potato. Transfer the remaining pork mixture to an airtight container; allow to cool, then store until needed (see tips).

TIPS

- We used an alcoholic apple cider; you can use a non-alcoholic one instead, if you like.
- Refrigerate the pork casserole for up to 3 days. Alternatively, freeze for up to 3 months; thaw in the fridge, then reheat in a microwave.

Indonesian-style chicken stew

DOUBLE BATCH | PREP + COOK TIME **1 HOUR 30 MINUTES** | SERVES **8**

Indonesian food is a melting pot of cultural influences gained over centuries from an array of arrivals who have contributed to the cuisine – Arab, Indian, Chinese, Spanish, British, and Dutch. The result is a varied and vibrant cuisine, and dishes such as the one here. Serve this with steamed rice, if you like.

1 bunch of coriander (100g)

2 long green chillies, seeded, finely chopped

¼ cup (60ml) kecap manis (sweet soy sauce; see tips)

6 garlic cloves, chopped

2 tbsp ginger paste

3 tsp Chinese five-spice powder

2 whole chickens (3.6kg)

1.5kg potatoes, halved or quartered, depending on size

1 tbsp extra virgin olive oil

1 chicken stock cube (10g), dissolved in 2 cups (500ml) boiling water

300g sugarsnap peas (see tips)

2 cups (240g) frozen garden peas

⅔ cup (100g) roasted cashews

salt and freshly ground black pepper

thinly sliced long green chilli, to serve (optional)

TIPS

- Kecap manis is sweetened with palm sugar or jaggery, giving it a molasses-like flavour.
- If you use whole chickens, freeze any unused bones or carcass to make your own chicken stock.
- Swap the sugarsnap peas for green beans, if green beans are cheaper.
- Refrigerate the stew in an airtight container for up to 2 days. Alternatively, freeze for up to 3 months; thaw in the fridge, then reheat in a microwave.

1   Preheat the oven to 200°C (180°C fan/400°F/Gas 6).

2   To make the marinade, wash and pick leaves from the coriander. Put the leaves in a medium bowl, cover with water; refrigerate until needed. Finely chop the coriander roots and stems; transfer to a large bowl. Add chilli, kecap manis, garlic, ginger, and five-spice; stir to combine.

3   Place the chickens, breast-side down, on a clean work surface. Use kitchen scissors to cut along either side of each backbone. Discard the backbones (or reserve for another use; see tips). Open the chickens; use a large, sharp knife to cut the breasts in half along the breastbone, cut off the wing tips and discard (or freeze with the backbones). Cut the chickens into serving-sized pieces by cutting around the legs to end up with 2 breast pieces and 2 chicken legs from each chicken. Add the chicken pieces to the bowl with the marinade; turn to coat each piece.

4   Put the potatoes and oil in a 7-litre cast-iron or other flameproof casserole. Season the chicken with salt and pepper to taste; add the chicken mixture to the dish with the stock. Bake, covered, for 50 minutes, turning the chicken halfway through the cooking time. Remove the lid; cook for a further 20 minutes or until the chicken is cooked through. Transfer the chicken and potatoes to a large plate or tray to keep warm. Strain the sauce through a fine sieve into a small heavy-based saucepan; simmer for 15 minutes or until the sauce is reduced by half. Return the chicken, potatoes, and sauce to the cleaned casserole.

5   Add the sugarsnap and garden peas to the dish; simmer for 2 minutes or until just cooked and the chicken and potatoes are heated through.

6   Serve half of the chicken stew topped with the cashews, drained reserved coriander leaves, and chilli, if you like. Transfer the remaining chicken stew to an airtight container; allow to cool, then store (see tips).

Lamb korma

VEGETARIAN SWAP | PREP + COOK TIME **30 MINUTES** | SERVES **4**

With roots in Mughlai cuisine, lamb korma is a fairly mild, rich curry. Its flavour is enhanced by the delicate use of spices such as nutmeg, saffron, and cardamom in the paste. Indeed, its emphasis should always be about the depth of flavour, rather than a burst of heat.

3 tbsp ghee or vegetable oil

800g lamb strips or diced lamb

1 large onion (200g), thinly sliced

2 garlic cloves, crushed

1 tbsp ginger paste

¼ cup (30g) ground almonds (see tips)

2 tsp poppy seeds

½ cup (150g) korma paste

½ cup (125ml) chicken stock

300ml double cream

⅓ cup (95g) Greek-style yogurt

1 cup (30g) coriander leaves

1   Heat 2 tablespoons of the ghee in a large saucepan; cook the lamb, in batches, until browned; remove from the pan.

2   Heat the remaining ghee in the same pan; cook the onion, garlic, and ginger paste, stirring, for a few minutes until the onion softens. Add the ground almonds, poppy seeds, and korma paste; cook, stirring, for a minute or two until fragrant.

3   Return the lamb to the pan with the chicken stock and cream; simmer, uncovered, for 15 minutes or until the sauce thickens slightly. Serve the korma accompanied by the yogurt and sprinkled with the coriander.

TIPS

- If you don't have ground almonds, make your own by blending or processing the same quantity of blanched whole almonds until finely ground. Make sure the nuts you use are as fresh as possible.
- For a vegetarian korma, swap the lamb for the same weight of paneer or tofu, and use vegetable stock instead of chicken.

Chicken wonton noodle soup

DO-AHEAD | PREP + COOK TIME **1 HOUR** | SERVES **4**

You can ad-lib the vegetables that you add to the soup, by choosing the best-priced one and according to the season, or by including any leftover fresh vegetables that may be lurking in the fridge. Other vegetables that work well here are: broccoli florets, sliced celery, sweetcorn, green beans, sugarsnap peas, and any leafy Asian-style greens.

2 tsp groundnut oil

2 garlic cloves, crushed

2 litres chicken stock

1 tbsp soy sauce

225g fresh egg noodles

800g baby pak choi, trimmed, halved or quartered lengthways

4 fresh shiitake mushrooms, trimmed, thinly sliced

4 spring onions, thinly sliced

chilli oil or chilli sauce, to serve (optional)

chicken wontons

150g chicken mince (see tips)

2 tbsp finely chopped water chestnuts

1 spring onion, finely chopped

1 garlic clove, finely chopped

1 tsp ginger paste

1 tsp sesame oil

1 tsp soy sauce, or to taste

16 wonton wrappers (see tips)

1 To make the chicken wontons, combine the chicken mince, water chestnuts, spring onion, garlic, ginger paste, sesame oil, and soy sauce in a bowl. Place 1 heaped teaspoon of the chicken mixture in the centre of each wonton wrapper. Brush the edges with water, then pinch together to seal. Cook the wontons, in batches, in a large saucepan of simmering water for 4 minutes or until cooked through. Remove with a slotted spoon onto a large tray. Set aside until needed.

2 Heat the groundnut oil in a large saucepan over a low heat; cook the garlic, stirring, for 2 minutes. Stir in the chicken stock, soy sauce, and 1 litre water; bring to the boil. Reduce the heat to low; simmer for 15 minutes.

3 Meanwhile, cook the egg noodles in a saucepan of boiling water according to the packet directions until tender; drain. Divide evenly among 4 serving bowls.

4 Add the pak choi and mushrooms to the soup; cook for 4 minutes or until the pak choi is tender but still crisp. Add the cooked wontons to the soup to warm through. Divide the wontons, vegetables, and soup evenly among the bowls.

5 Serve the soup sprinkled with the spring onions and a drizzle of chilli oil, if you like; season with extra soy sauce, if needed.

TIPS

- Use pork mince instead of chicken, if you like.
- Look for wonton wrappers in the freezer section of Asian supermarkets or speciality grocers.
- Uncooked wontons can be frozen in an airtight container, in single layers separated by sheets of baking parchment, for up to 2 months.

Chicken and chorizo gumbo

DOUBLE BATCH | PREP + COOK TIME **2 HOURS 30 MINUTES + STANDING** | SERVES **6**

The punchily flavoured Creole-Cajun soup hailing from Louisiana and known as gumbo has West African origins. Now very much a signature dish, family recipes for gumbo can be closely guarded. Traditionally, it is thickened with okra or filé, the dried powdered leaves of the sassafras tree; in lieu of this not-so-easily found ingredient, a little more flour is added here.

50g butter

2 cured chorizo sausages (340g), thickly sliced on the diagonal (see tips)

1.5kg chicken thighs, bone in, skin removed, excess fat trimmed

1 onion (150g), chopped

2–3 red peppers (400g), cut into 4cm pieces

1 tbsp Cajun seasoning

2 tbsp plain flour

3 cups (750ml) chicken stock

400g can diced tomatoes

200g fresh or frozen okra

2 bay leaves

1 cup (200g) white long-grain rice or basmati rice, rinsed

flat-leaf parsley leaves, to serve

1 Melt the butter in a 6.75-litre cast-iron or other flameproof casserole over a medium-high heat. Cook the chorizo for 3 minutes on each side or until browned; transfer to a large heatproof bowl.

2 Cook the chicken in the same casserole, turning, for 8 minutes or until golden all over; transfer to the bowl with the chorizo.

3 Now add the onion to the casserole; cook, stirring, for 5 minutes or until softened. Add the red peppers and Cajun seasoning; cook, stirring, for 1 minute or until fragrant. Add the flour to make a roux; cook, stirring, for 30 seconds or until the mixture looks dry.

4 Gradually stir in the chicken stock, then the diced tomatoes, okra, and bay leaves. Return the chicken and chorizo to the dish; bring to the boil. Reduce the heat to low; cook, covered, for 1 hour. Stir in the rice; cook, covered, for a further 15 minutes or until the rice is cooked. Allow to stand for 10 minutes.

5 Serve half of the gumbo topped with parsley. Transfer the remaining gumbo to an airtight container; allow to cool, then store until needed (see tip).

TIPS

• Andouille sausage, a French smoked pork sausage, is traditionally used in both gumbo and jambalaya, but chorizo makes a good substitute.

• Refrigerate the gumbo in an airtight container for up to 2 days. Alternatively, freeze for up to 3 months; thaw in the fridge, then reheat in a microwave.

Creamy rosemary and mustard chicken

DOUBLE BATCH | PREP + COOK TIME **1 HOUR 40 MINUTES** | SERVES **6**

A great way to create an easy midweek meal, this chicken casserole will warm you up from the inside out with its tempting amalgam of sweet honey and bitey mustard. Parsnips have quite a long season over autumn to spring, but are at their sweetest during winter.

¼ cup (60ml) olive oil

6 chicken legs (about 2kg), bone in, skin on

2 onions (450g), thinly sliced

6 garlic cloves, thinly sliced

½ cup (125ml) brandy

2 chicken stock cubes (20g), crumbled

2 tbsp wholegrain mustard

¼ cup (90g) runny honey

4 large sprigs of fresh rosemary, plus extra 2 tsp finely chopped rosemary leaves

8 parsnips (2kg), halved lengthways

200ml crème fraîche or soured cream

salt and freshly ground black pepper

TIP

Refrigerate the chicken casserole and parsnips in separate containers for up to 2 days. Alternatively, freeze for up to 3 months; thaw in the fridge, then reheat in a microwave.

1 Preheat the oven to 180°C (160°C fan/350°F/Gas 4).

2 Heat 1 tablespoon of the olive oil in a 7-litre flameproof roasting tin over a high heat. Season the chicken with salt and pepper to taste; cook half of the chicken for 4 minutes on each side or until well browned. Transfer to a plate. Repeat with another tablespoon of the olive oil and the remaining chicken. Discard any excess oil in the tin.

3 Add the onion and garlic to the same tin; cook, stirring, for 5 minutes or until softened. Add the brandy; cook, scraping the bottom of the tin to loosen any caramelized bits. Stir in the stock cubes, 2½ cups (625ml) water, mustard, honey, and rosemary sprigs; bring to the boil. Return the chicken to the tin. Cover the surface of the chicken with baking parchment, then cover the tin tightly with 2 layers of foil.

4 Transfer to the oven; bake for 40 minutes or until the chicken is cooked through. Remove the foil and paper; return to the oven for a further 15 minutes or until the chicken is golden and cooked through.

5 Meanwhile, arrange the parsnips on a baking tray lined with baking parchment; rub with the remaining olive oil, sprinkle with the extra 2 teaspoons chopped rosemary, then season with salt and pepper to taste. Roast alongside the chicken for the last 40 minutes of the cooking time or until the parsnips are golden and tender, rotating the tray halfway through to ensure the parsnips cook evenly.

6 Transfer the chicken to a large plate; separate the drumsticks and thighs, if you like. Skim off and discard any excess fat from the surface of the sauce. Whisk in the crème fraîche; simmer over a medium heat for 2 minutes or until heated through. Return the chicken to the tin.

7 Serve half of the chicken casserole with half of the parsnips. Transfer the remaining chicken casserole and parsnips to separate airtight containers; allow to cool, then store until needed (see tip).

Pork adobo

DO-AHEAD | PREP + COOK TIME **55 MINUTES + STANDING** | SERVES **6**

This classic Filipino dish of braised pork is tangy, slightly sweet, and rich with umami undertones from the soy sauce. It can be made with other cuts of meat such as chicken, but the piquant sauce works particularly well with pork.

800g pork loin fillets, thickly sliced across the grain

$\frac{1}{3}$ cup (80ml) apple cider vinegar

$\frac{1}{3}$ cup (80ml) light soy sauce

2 bay leaves

3 garlic cloves, crushed

2 tsp ginger paste

1 tbsp vegetable oil

1 beef stock cube (10g), crumbled

2 tbsp oyster sauce

1 orange sweet potato (400g), thickly sliced

200g baby green beans, trimmed

1$\frac{1}{4}$ cups (250g) white long-grain rice

400g can black beans, drained, rinsed

$\frac{1}{2}$ cup (25g) coarsely chopped coriander, plus extra sprigs, to serve (optional)

salt and freshly ground black pepper

1 Put the pork, apple cider vinegar, soy sauce, bay leaves, garlic, and ginger paste in a large bowl; season with salt and pepper to taste. Stir to coat; refrigerate for 30 minutes to allow the flavours to develop.

2 Drain the pork; reserve the marinade. Heat the vegetable oil in a flameproof casserole or large heavy-based saucepan over a high heat; cook half of the pork mixture, stirring, for 5 minutes or until browned all over. Transfer to a plate. Repeat with the remaining pork mixture.

3 Add the reserved marinade, stock cube, 2 cups (500ml) water, and oyster sauce to the dish; stir in the sweet potato. Bring to the boil. Reduce the heat to medium; cook, covered, for 20 minutes or until the pork and sweet potato are tender. Stir in the green beans; cook, covered, for 2 minutes or until the beans are just tender. Cook, uncovered, over a high heat for 3 minutes or until the sauce is thickened and glossy.

4 Meanwhile, put the rice and 1$\frac{3}{4}$ cups (430ml) water in a heavy-based saucepan; bring to the boil. Reduce the heat to low; cook, covered for 12 minutes or until the water is absorbed and the rice is tender. Stir in the black beans and the $\frac{1}{2}$ cup (25g) chopped coriander.

5 Serve the pork adobo with the black bean rice and sprinkled with extra sprigs of coriander, if you like.

TIP

The pork can be prepared to the end of step 1 the day before, and marinated in the fridge overnight.

Hungarian goulash soup

DO-AHEAD | PREP + COOK TIME **2 HOURS 45 MINUTES** | SERVES **4**

While not traditional, pre-prepared gnocchi (potato dumplings) have been included as a convenient stand-in for the usual accompaniment of spaetzle (a small, rustically formed noodle) in this substantial, winter-warming soup-cum-stew.

2 tbsp olive oil

40g butter

900g boneless veal shoulder, coarsely chopped (see tips)

2 onions (300g), finely chopped

1 tbsp tomato purée

1 tbsp plain flour

1 tbsp sweet paprika

1 tsp caraway seeds

$1/2$ tsp cayenne pepper

2 garlic cloves, crushed

1 litre beef stock

400g canned chopped tomatoes

2 red peppers (350g), thinly sliced

250g premade potato gnocchi

salt and freshly ground black pepper

chervil or flat-leaf parsley, to serve (optional)

1 Heat 1 tablespoon of the olive oil and half of the butter in a large heavy-based saucepan over a medium-high heat; cook the veal, in batches, for 5 minutes or until browned all over. Remove from the pan.

2 Heat the remaining 1 tablespoon olive oil and remaining butter in the same pan over a medium heat; cook the onions, stirring, for 5 minutes or until softened.

3 Add the tomato purée, flour, sweet paprika, caraway seeds, cayenne pepper, and garlic to the pan; cook, stirring, for 2 minutes. Return the veal to the pan with 2 cups (500ml) water, beef stock, and tomatoes; bring to the boil. Reduce the heat to low; simmer for $2^{1}/_{2}$ hours. Add the red peppers; cook for a further 10 minutes or until peppers and beef are tender. Season with salt and pepper to taste.

4 Meanwhile, cook the gnocchi in a large saucepan of boiling water until the gnocchi floats to the surface; drain.

5 Serve the goulash soup with the gnocchi and a sprinkling of chervil, if you like.

TIPS

▪ You can swap beef chuck or blade steak for the veal, if you like.

▪ This dish is a cross between a soup and a stew; if a thinner soup is preferred, cook for $1^{1}/_{2}$ hours at step 3, and thin with boiling water or extra warmed stock to the desired consistency.

▪ The soup is suitable for freezing at the end of step 3. Thaw the soup in the fridge overnight; reheat the soup and cook the gnocchi just before serving.

Chicken tagine with dates and honey

DOUBLE BATCH | PREP + COOK TIME **2 HOURS** | SERVES **8**

A little bit sweet, a little bit savoury, and a whole lot delicious, this simple chicken tagine can be served as either a midweek family dinner or a special-occasion dish – or both, as this is a double-batch recipe where half can be stored to use at another time.

1/4 cup (60ml) olive oil

2kg chicken thigh fillets, cut into pieces

4 onions (600g), thinly sliced

4 garlic cloves, crushed

2 1/2 tbsp ras el hanout (see tips)

3 cups (750ml) chicken stock

3/4 cup (105g) pitted dates, halved

1/4 cup (90g) runny honey

3/4 cup (120g) blanched almonds, toasted, coarsely chopped

coriander sprigs, to serve (optional)

plain couscous or Lemon Pistachio Couscous (see page 26), to serve

1   Heat half of the olive oil in a 7-litre cast-iron or other flameproof casserole over a medium-high heat. Cook the chicken in batches, stirring, for 5 minutes or until browned all over; transfer each batch of chicken to a large heatproof bowl.

2   Heat the remaining olive oil in the same dish; cook the onions, garlic, and ras el hanout, stirring, for 5 minutes or until the onions soften. Return the chicken to the dish, then add the stock and 1 1/2 cups (375ml) water; bring to a simmer.

3   Cook, covered, over a low heat for 1 hour, stirring occasionally. Remove the lid; continue cooking, uncovered, over a low-medium heat for a further 30 minutes or until the sauce thickens slightly and the chicken is tender. Stir in the dates and honey.

4   Serve half of the chicken tagine topped with the almonds and coriander, if you like, accompanied by the couscous. Transfer the remaining chicken tagine to an airtight container; cool, then store (see tips).

TIPS

▪ North Africa's ras el hanout – its name means "head of shop", or "top shelf" – is made up of more than a dozen spices. Traditionally its makeup and proportions vary from one merchant to another, but it is always subtly savoury with a touch of heat.

▪ The quantity of blanched almonds is enough for the served chicken tagine. Use the same amount again when serving the stored portion.

▪ Refrigerate the chicken tagine for up to 2 days. Alternatively, freeze for up to 3 months; thaw in the fridge, then reheat in a microwave.

BAKES, PIES, AND ROASTS

Hankering for pan-baked temptations oozing with goodness, sticky barbecue or succulent braises, maybe a comforting pie guaranteed to soothe and succour? Look no further.

Sausage agrodolce and polenta bake

VEGETARIAN SWAP | PREP + COOK TIME **1 HOUR** | SERVES **4**

Soft polenta is deliciously unctuous and works well with the sweet-and-sour flavours of this Italian-inspired dish, making it the perfect bake for a cool-weather dinner. For an equally moreish vegetarian version, see our tips.

¹/₃ cup (80ml) olive oil

500g chipolata sausages (see tips)

3 finger aubergines (180g), halved lengthways

350g mini red peppers, seeded, sliced lengthways (see tips)

2 garlic cloves, crushed

1 tsp fennel seeds

2 tbsp tomato purée

¹/₄ cup (60ml) balsamic vinegar

3 tsp caster sugar

¹/₃ cup (60g) green olives

¹/₃ cup (25g) finely grated Parmesan or pecorino or other cheese of your choice

¹/₄ cup (7g) small flat-leaf parsley leaves

soft polenta

1 cup (170g) polenta

¹/₂ cup (125ml) double cream

50g butter, chopped

¹/₃ cup (25g) finely grated Parmesan or pecorino or other cheese of your choice

salt and freshly ground black pepper

TIPS

- For a vegetarian option, swap the chipolatas for vegetarian sausages and choose a cheese made with vegetarian rennet.
- We used mini sweet peppers, but if you cannot find them use 2 sliced medium red peppers instead.

1 Heat 2 teaspoons of the olive oil in a large deep frying pan over a medium heat. Add the sausages; cook, turning, for 10 minutes or until browned all over. Transfer to a plate lined with kitchen paper. Set aside.

2 Add ¹/₄ cup (60ml) of the olive oil to the pan; cook the aubergines, stirring, for 8 minutes or until lightly browned. Using a slotted spoon, transfer to a bowl. Add the remaining 2 teaspoons olive oil to the pan; cook the peppers, stirring, for 5 minutes or until softened. Stir in the garlic and fennel seeds; cook for 2 minutes. Stir in the tomato purée and return the aubergines to the pan; cook for a further 1 minute.

3 Add the balsamic vinegar, caster sugar, and ¹/₂ cup (125ml) water; bring to the boil. Reduce the heat to low; cook, covered, for 10 minutes or until the mixture is thickened and slightly reduced.

4 Meanwhile, to make the soft polenta, bring 3 cups (750ml) water to the boil in a heavy-based 2.5-litre (10-cup) flameproof roasting tin over a high heat. Gradually add the polenta in a thin, steady stream, whisking continuously until all the polenta is incorporated into the water; reduce the heat to low. Cook, stirring continuously with a wooden spoon, for 12 minutes or until the mixture thickens and the polenta is soft. Remove from the heat; stir in the cream, butter, and cheese until well combined. Season with salt and pepper to taste.

5 Preheat the oven to 200°C (180°C fan/400°F/Gas 6).

6 Spoon the sausages and aubergine mixture evenly over the polenta, top with the olives and cheese; bake for 10 minutes. Sprinkle with the parsley before serving.

Cottage pie

DO-AHEAD | PREP + COOK TIME **1 HOUR 30 MINUTES** | SERVES **4**

A cosy classic, cottage pie is simple to make and comforting to eat. A great stand-by for weeknight suppers or to ward off the chill of a winter's night, it is also a way of stretching a few simple ingredients just that little bit further – with no skimping on satisfaction.

2 tsp olive oil

1kg beef mince

1 brown onion (150g), finely chopped

1 carrot (120g), finely sliced

1 trimmed celery stick (100g), finely sliced

1 tbsp chopped thyme leaves, plus extra sprigs, to serve (optional)

1 cup (250ml) beef stock

1 tbsp Worcestershire sauce

1/4 cup (70g) tomato purée

400g canned diced tomatoes

1/2 cup (60g) frozen garden peas

2 tbsp grated Cheddar

mashed potato topping

6 floury or all-purpose potatoes (1.2kg), coarsely chopped (see tips)

60g butter

1/4 cup (60ml) milk

1 Preheat the oven to 180°C (160°C fan/350°F/Gas 4).

2 Heat the olive oil in a large saucepan over a high heat; cook the beef and onion, stirring, for 5 minutes or until browned.

3 Add the carrot, celery, thyme, beef stock, Worcestershire sauce, tomato purée, and tomatoes; simmer, uncovered, for 30 minutes or until the carrots are tender. Add the garden peas; cook for 10 minutes or until the peas are tender and the liquid has thickened.

4 Meanwhile, to make the mashed potato topping, boil, steam, or microwave the potatoes until tender; drain. Mash the potatoes with the butter and milk until light and fluffy.

5 Spoon the beef mixture into a 2.5-litre (10-cup) ovenproof dish. Spread the mashed potato topping over the beef mixture; sprinkle with the cheese. Bake, uncovered, for 30 minutes or until the pie is heated through and the topping is golden. Serve sprinkled with extra sprigs of thyme, if you like.

TIPS

• For the perfect mashed topping to this pie, choose a mashing potato such as King Edward or Maris Piper for the fluffiest mashed potato, and make sure to salt the cooking water.

• You can prepare the recipe a day ahead, cover, and refrigerate until ready to cook. You will need to add an extra 10–15 minutes to the cooking time.

Jerk pork cutlets with butternut chips

FAST COOK | PREP + COOK TIME **45 MINUTES** | SERVES **4**

In culinary terms, "jerk" refers to a Jamaican style of cooking where spicy seasoning is used to marinate meat, seafood, or poultry before grilling. While each cook has their particular favourite combination of spices, jerk almost always contains allspice, thyme, and chilli.

3 long green chillies, coarsely chopped

3 spring onions, coarsely chopped

2 garlic cloves, crushed

1 tsp ground allspice

1 tsp dried thyme

1 tsp white granulated sugar

1 tbsp soy sauce

1 tbsp lime juice

4 x 280g pork loin chops

1kg piece of butternut squash, trimmed

2 tbsp vegetable oil

peri-peri mayonnaise

1/3 cup (100g) mayonnaise

2 tbsp peri-peri sauce

1 Combine the chillies, spring onions, garlic, allspice, thyme, sugar, soy sauce, lime juice, and pork in a medium bowl.

2 To make the peri-peri mayonnaise, combine the ingredients in a small bowl. Set aside.

3 Cut the butternut squash into 7cm chips; boil, steam, or microwave until tender. Drain; combine the chips with the vegetable oil in a medium bowl. Cook the chips on a preheated ridged cast-iron grill pan over a medium-high heat. Set aside to keep warm.

4 Cook the pork on the same preheated pan for 4 minutes on each side or until cooked through.

5 Serve the pork with the butternut chips and peri-peri mayonnaise.

TIP

You can swap the pork for skinless boneless chicken breasts, if you like.

Chicken and sweetcorn enchilada bake

VEGETARIAN SWAP | PREP + COOK TIME **1 HOUR** | SERVES **4**

Canned tomatoes serve a dual role in this hunger-busting dish, as the simple salsa topping for the enchiladas and as the base for their smoky chicken and sweetcorn filling. Add in the layer of melting cheese over the top and you have a real crowd-pleaser on your hands.

2 trimmed sweetcorn cobs (500g)

2 tbsp olive oil

500g skinless boneless chicken breasts, thinly sliced (see tips)

1 red onion (170g), finely chopped

2 garlic cloves, crushed

1 long green chilli, chopped (optional)

3 tsp smoked paprika

1½ tsp ground cumin

2 x 400g cans diced tomatoes (see tips)

1 tbsp lime or lemon juice

8 x 20cm flour tortillas

2 cups (240g) coarsely grated Cheddar

¼ cup (7g) coriander leaves

salt and freshly ground black pepper

lime or lemon wedges and soured cream, to serve

1   Preheat the oven to 220°C (200°C fan/425°F/Gas 7).

2   Brush the sweetcorn with 1 tablespoon of the olive oil. Heat a ridged cast-iron grill pan to a high heat; cook the sweetcorn, turning occasionally, for 10 minutes or until golden and tender. Cut the kernels from the cobs, in sections if possible; discard the cobs.

3   Meanwhile, heat the remaining olive oil in a large heavy-based frying pan over a high heat. Cook the chicken, onion, garlic, half of the chilli (if using), smoked paprika, and cumin, stirring, for 7 minutes or until browned. Add half of the tomatoes. Bring to a simmer; cook for 10 minutes. Add the lime juice and half of the corn; season with salt and pepper to taste.

4   Place the tortillas on a clean work surface. Spoon the chicken mixture evenly along the centre of each tortilla. Divide 1 cup (120g) of the Cheddar evenly among the tortillas; fold to enclose the filling. Place, join-side down, in a single layer, in an oiled 20cm x 30cm ovenproof dish. Spoon over the remaining tomatoes, leaving the ends of the tortillas exposed; sprinkle with the remaining Cheddar.

5   Bake for 15 minutes or until golden. Sprinkle the enchiladas with the remaining sweetcorn, coriander, and chilli (if using); serve with lime wedges and soured cream.

TIPS

• To make the recipe even faster, use chicken or pork mince instead of sliced breast fillets.

• You can substitute a jar of salsa for one of the cans of diced tomatoes to top the dish, if you like.

• To make this vegetarian, omit the chicken and add a 400g can drained and rinsed kidney beans and a 400g can drained and rinsed black beans in step 3 when adding the tomatoes. And make sure you use vegetarian Cheddar.

Moroccan-spiced moussaka bake

DOUBLE BATCH | PREP + COOK TIME **3 HOURS** | SERVES **8**

This recipe takes inspiration from a Greek moussaka and adds a twist with harissa paste for a spicy edge and kidney beans for what is all in all a wholesome and filling bake. Lamb is the traditional choice for moussaka, but beef stands up to the strong flavours here equally well.

1 tbsp olive oil

2 red onions (340g), thinly sliced

3 garlic cloves, thinly sliced

1.5kg lamb or beef mince

2$\frac{1}{2}$ tbsp harissa paste

400g can cherry or chopped tomatoes

2 x 400g cans red kidney beans, drained, rinsed

$\frac{1}{2}$ cup (125ml) vegetable stock

1 red pepper (200g), thinly sliced

2 aubergines (600g), cut into 1cm thick rounds

2 cups (140g) coarse wholemeal breadcrumbs

cooking oil spray

$\frac{1}{2}$ cup (15g) flat-leaf parsley leaves

lemon and herb yogurt

1 cup (280g) Greek-style yogurt

1 cup (30g) firmly packed flat-leaf parsley leaves

$\frac{1}{4}$ cup (5g) tarragon or mint leaves

2 tbsp lemon juice

salt and freshly ground black pepper

1 Preheat the oven to 180°C (160°C fan/350°F/Gas 4).

2 Heat the olive oil in a 6.75-litre cast-iron or other flameproof casserole over a high heat. Cook the onions, stirring, for 4 minutes or until softened and golden. Add the garlic; cook, stirring, for 1 minute.

3 Add the lamb mince; cook, stirring to break up any clumps, for 10 minutes or until browned. Add the harissa paste; cook, stirring, for 30 seconds or until well combined. Reduce the heat to low.

4 Add the tomatoes, kidney beans, and vegetable stock to the dish; top with half of the red pepper. Arrange the aubergines, slightly overlapping and in concentric circles, on top to cover the surface. Top with the remaining red pepper. Cover with a tight-fitting lid. Transfer the dish to the oven; bake for 1$\frac{1}{2}$ hours or until the aubergines soften. Sprinkle the breadcrumbs over the aubergine layer; spray with cooking oil. Return to the oven; bake, uncovered, for a further 20 minutes or until the breadcrumbs are golden.

5 Meanwhile, to make the lemon and herb yogurt, pulse half of the yogurt with the herbs and lemon juice in a small food processor until smooth. Transfer to a small bowl; stir in the remaining yogurt. Season with salt and pepper to taste.

6 Serve half of the moussaka topped with the parsley and accompanied by the lemon and herb yogurt. Transfer the remaining moussaka to an airtight container; allow to cool, then store until needed (see tip).

TIP

Refrigerate the moussaka for up to 2 days. Alternatively, freeze for up to 3 months; thaw in the fridge, then reheat in a microwave.

Crunchy buttermilk chicken

FAMILY FAVOURITE | PREP + COOK TIME **1 HOUR** | SERVES **4**

The secret to this crunchy yet succulent chicken recipe is in the coating made with cornflakes, which results in a tantalizing crumb coating. To make this recipe gluten-free, use gluten-free cornflakes and rice flour instead of the plain flour.

5^1/$_2$ cups (220g) cornflakes

1^1/$_2$ tbsp finely chopped thyme

^{1}/$_3$ cup (50g) plain flour

1 tsp paprika

1 tsp garlic powder

1 tsp sea salt flakes

^{1}/$_2$ tsp ground black pepper

^{3}/$_4$ cup (185ml) buttermilk

8 chicken drumsticks (about 1.2kg), skin removed

4 streaky bacon rashers

2 sweetcorn cobs (800g), trimmed, halved

80g mixed salad leaves

1 Preheat the oven to 200°C (180°C fan/400°F/Gas 6).

2 Put the cornflakes in a large resealable plastic bag; crush with a rolling pin until coarsely crumbed. Combine the cornflake crumbs and thyme in a medium bowl.

3 Combine the flour, paprika, garlic powder, sea salt flakes, and black pepper in a shallow bowl. Pour the buttermilk into another shallow bowl.

4 Coat the drumsticks in the flour mixture, shake off any excess. Dip the drumsticks in the buttermilk, then dip in the cornflake mixture, turning until covered all over.

5 Arrange the drumsticks in a single layer on a large baking tray lined with baking parchment; roast for 40 minutes or until cooked through.

6 Meanwhile, wrap a bacon rasher around the middle of each of the pieces of sweetcorn; secure the ends with a toothpick or cocktail stick. Season with salt and pepper to taste.

7 Arrange the sweetcorn on a separate baking tray; roast for the last 20 minutes of the chicken cooking time.

8 Serve the chicken and sweetcorn with salad leaves.

TIPS

- Ask your butcher or poultry supplier to remove the skin from the chicken for you, if you like.
- If the chicken is getting too brown during roasting, cover the tray with foil.

Sauces and gravy

A home-made sauce can be that little extra touch that elevates a meal from the everyday to the extraordinary. Our recipes involve only a little preparation, but the results are full of fresh flavours and are sure to make dinner something special.

Sage and onion gravy

PREP + COOK TIME **20 MINUTES** | SERVES **4**

Heat 2 tablespoons olive oil in a medium saucepan over a medium-high heat; cook 1 small crushed garlic clove and ½ cup (80g) caramelized onion for 1 minute or until fragrant. Add 1 tablespoon plain flour; cook, stirring, for 1 minute. Gradually add 1 cup (250ml) chicken or beef stock, then 8 torn sage leaves and ⅓ cup (80ml) cider; simmer for 10 minutes or until the gravy is slightly thickened. Season with salt and freshly ground black pepper to taste.

Creamy mushroom sauce

PREP + COOK TIME **15 MINUTES** | SERVES **4**

Melt 40g butter in a heavy-based frying pan over a medium-high heat; cook 400g sliced button mushrooms, stirring, until browned. Add 1 crushed garlic clove; stir for 1 minute. Stir in ¾ cup (185ml) beef stock and ¾ cup (185ml) double cream; simmer until slightly thickened. Stir in 2 tablespoons finely chopped flat-leaf parsley. Season with salt and freshly ground black pepper to taste.

Mint sauce

PREP + COOK TIME **10 MINUTES + STANDING** | MAKES **1 CUP**

Put 1 cup (25g) firmly packed mint leaves in a heatproof bowl. Stir ¾ cup (185ml) white wine vinegar, ¼ cup (60ml) water, and 2 tablespoons white granulated sugar in a heavy-based saucepan over a low heat, without boiling, until the sugar dissolves; pour over the mint. Cover; allow to stand for 3 hours. Strain the liquid into a jug; discard the mint. Add 1 cup (25g) firmly packed mint leaves to the liquid; blend or process until finely chopped.

Mango chutney yogurt

PREP + COOK TIME **5 MINUTES** | MAKES **1¼ CUPS**

Combine 1 cup (280g) Greek-style yogurt and 2 teaspoons lemon juice in a small bowl; season with salt and freshly ground black pepper to taste. Swirl through 2 tablespoons mango chutney. Season with freshly ground pepper, and top with coriander leaves before serving, if you like.

Chicken and thyme one-pan pie

DO-AHEAD | PREP + COOK TIME **1 HOUR + COOLING** | SERVES **4**

When you're cold, tired, and looking for something comforting to satisfy hungry appetites, it's hard to go past this beautifully simple and wonderfully fragrant chicken pie, cooked all in the one dish for ease. Serve with broccolini (Tenderstem broccoli) or other seasonal greens.

800g chicken thigh fillets, thinly sliced

2 tbsp olive oil

1 large leek (500g), thinly sliced

2 garlic cloves, crushed

1 tbsp thyme leaves, plus extra sprigs, to serve

$1/2$ cup (70g) slivered almonds

$1/4$ cup (35g) plain flour

2 chicken stock cubes (20g), dissolved in 3 cups (750ml) boiling water

2 sheets of puff pastry

1 egg, lightly beaten

salt and freshly ground black pepper

1. Preheat the oven to 200°C (180°C fan/400°F/Gas 6).

2. Season the chicken with salt and pepper to taste. Heat the olive oil in a 25cm (top measurement), 19cm (base measurement) ovenproof frying pan over a high heat; cook the chicken, in batches, stirring occasionally, for 3 minutes or until browned. Remove the chicken from the pan.

3. Cook the leek in the same pan, stirring occasionally, for 3 minutes or until softened. Add the garlic, thyme, and almonds; cook, stirring, for 1 minute or until fragrant. Return the chicken to the pan with the flour; cook, stirring, for 1 minute. Gradually stir in the chicken stock; bring to the boil. Reduce the heat to low-medium; simmer, stirring occasionally, for 5 minutes or until thickened slightly. Season with salt and pepper to taste. Allow to cool for 10 minutes.

4. Trim the pastry to fit the top of the pan. Cut the pastry offcuts into decorative shapes. Top the pie with the pastry shapes; brush with the beaten egg to glaze.

5. Bake the pie for 20 minutes or until the pastry is golden. Serve topped with extra sprigs of thyme.

TIPS

- The filling can be made, covered, and refrigerated up to 2 days ahead.
- The baked pie can be frozen for up to 3 months if made (and then stored) in an ovenproof dish; thaw in the fridge before reheating.

Red-cooked pork

PREP + COOK TIME **1 HOUR 10 MINUTES** | SERVES **8**

The Chinese method of "red cooking", a slow-braising technique that imparts a reddish hue to the meat, is ideal for cuts such as boneless pork shoulder. Pork butt is another popular choice for this method, as it becomes meltingly tender after long, slow cooking.

1.6kg piece of boneless shoulder of pork, rind removed, excess fat trimmed

2 cups (500ml) Shaoxing rice wine or dry sherry

3 cups (750ml) light soy sauce

1 tbsp ginger paste

8 spring onions

6 star anise

4 cinnamon sticks

1 cup (220g) soft brown sugar

1/3 cup (120g) runny honey

steamed vegetables and sliced red chilli, to serve

1 Tie the pork with kitchen string at 2cm intervals, to form a compact shape; this helps the pork to cook evenly.

2 Heat a 6.75-litre cast-iron or other flameproof casserole over a high heat. Cook the pork, turning, for 8 minutes or until browned all over; transfer to a large plate or tray.

3 Add 1 litre water to the dish with the rice wine, soy sauce, ginger paste, spring onions, star anise, cinnamon, and sugar; bring to the boil over a high heat. Reduce the heat to medium; simmer for 30 minutes or until the liquid is reduced by one-third.

4 Return the pork to the dish; cook, covered, turning occasionally, over a medium heat for 50 minutes or until the pork is tender. Transfer the pork to a tray. Strain the cooking liquid into a heatproof jug; discard the solids.

5 Put 3 cups (750ml) of the strained cooking liquid into a heavy-based saucepan; stir in the honey. Bring to the boil over a high heat; simmer for 15 minutes or until the liquid is reduced to the consistency of a slightly sticky sauce.

6 Cut the pork into thick slices. Serve half of the pork with half of the sauce, accompanied by steamed vegetables and red chilli. Transfer the remaining pork and sauce to an airtight container; allow to cool, then store until needed (see tips).

TIPS

- Refrigerate the pork and sauce for up to 3 days. Alternatively, freeze for up to 3 months; thaw in the fridge, then reheat in a microwave.
- Freeze the remaining cooking liquid in batches for another use, if you like (this is often kept and used as a master stock in Chinese cooking).

Chicken parmigiana

DOUBLE BATCH | PREP + COOK TIME **1 HOUR 45 MINUTES** | SERVES **6**

This crumb topping is a great opportunity to use up any day-old bread, while the Parmesan can easily be replaced with any leftover pieces of cheese on hand in the fridge. Serve the parmigiana with a simple green salad, if you like, for a balanced meal.

12 chicken thigh fillets (about 2kg), excess fat trimmed

12 thin slices of prosciutto or ham (180g)

2 tbsp olive oil

1 large onion (200g), finely chopped

3 garlic cloves, crushed

$^1/_2$ cup (125ml) dry white wine

4 x 400g jars tomato and chilli pasta sauce

2 tbsp finely chopped oregano leaves, plus extra leaves, to serve

175g Italian-style bread, coarsely torn

$^1/_2$ cup (15g) finely chopped flat-leaf parsley

$^1/_2$ cup (40g) finely grated Parmesan

60g butter, melted

salt and freshly ground black pepper

1 Preheat the oven to 160°C (140°C fan/325°F/Gas 3).

2 Season the chicken with salt and pepper to taste; wrap each thigh in a slice of prosciutto.

3 Heat the olive oil in a 4-litre flameproof roasting tin over a medium-high heat. Cook the chicken, seam-side down, for 4 minutes or until golden. Turn, then cook for another 4 minutes or until golden all over; transfer to a large plate or tray. Set aside.

4 Add the onion to the tin; cook, stirring, for 3 minutes or until softened. Next, add the garlic; cook, stirring, for 30 seconds or until fragrant. Pour in the wine; cook, stirring, for 1 minute or until slightly reduced.

5 Return the chicken to the tin in a single layer. Pour the pasta sauce over the chicken and sprinkle with the 2 tablespoons finely chopped oregano; season with salt and pepper to taste. Cover the tin tightly with baking parchment and 2 layers of foil; bake for 40 minutes.

6 Meanwhile, process the bread to form coarse crumbs. Combine the breadcrumbs, parsley, Parmesan, and butter in a bowl.

7 Remove the foil and baking parchment from the tin; sprinkle the chicken with the breadcrumb mixture. Bake, uncovered, for a further 30 minutes or until the crumb mixture is golden.

8 Serve half of the chicken parmigiana topped with the extra oregano leaves. Transfer the remaining chicken parmigiana to an airtight container; allow to cool, then store until needed (see tip).

TIP

Refrigerate the chicken parmigiana in an airtight container for up to 2 days. Alternatively, freeze for up to 3 months; thaw in the fridge, then reheat in a microwave.

Cuban beef empanadas

PREP + COOK TIME **1 HOUR 20 MINUTES + COOLING** | SERVES **4**

Serve these empanadas with a mixed-leaf avocado salad, if you like, or try them with the Balsamic Roasted Squash and Red Quinoa Salad on page 146.

$^1/_3$ cup (80ml) olive oil

1 red onion (170g), finely chopped

3 garlic cloves, finely chopped

1 cured chorizo sausage (170g), finely diced

1 large red pepper (350g), finely chopped

500g beef mince

2 tsp ground cumin

2 tsp smoked paprika

$^1/_4$ cup (40g) currants

400g can diced tomatoes

1 tbsp tomato purée

8 ready-rolled sheets of shortcrust pastry (400g)

1kg butternut squash, peeled, cut into 2cm pieces

$^1/_2$ tsp ground cinnamon

1 egg, lightly beaten

2 tbsp polenta

salt and freshly ground black pepper

lime wedges and chilli sauce, to serve

TIPS

• This makes 8 empanadas. If you have any left over, store in an airtight container in the fridge for up to 2 days; warm in a preheated 180°C (160°C fan/350°F/Gas 4) oven. Or wrap individually in cling film, then freeze in an airtight container for up to 1 month.

• For a spicy shepherd's pie, use lamb mince instead of beef. Put the filling in a medium ovenproof dish, top with mashed potato or sweet potato, and bake at the same temperature for 30 minutes or until lightly browned. Serve with your favourite chilli sauce.

1 Preheat the oven to 180°C (160°C fan/350°F/Gas 4). Line a large baking tray with baking parchment.

2 Heat 2 tablespoons of the olive oil in a large heavy-based frying pan over a high heat. Add the onion; cook for 3 minutes or until softened. Add the garlic, chorizo, and red pepper; cook, stirring, for 4 minutes or until the pepper is softened.

3 Add the beef mince to the pan; cook, stirring with a wooden spoon to break up any clumps, for 10 minutes or until browned.

4 Stir in the cumin and smoked paprika; cook for 1 minute or until aromatic. Add the currants, tomatoes, tomato purée, and $^1/_2$ cup (125ml) water. Bring to the boil; cook for 10 minutes or until most of the liquid is evaporated and the mixture is thickened. Allow to cool.

5 Cut eight 25cm squares of baking parchment. Cut an 18cm round from each pastry sheet; place each one on a piece of baking parchment.

6 Place an eighth of the beef filling in the centre of each pastry round. Brush a little of the beaten egg around the edge of the pastry. Fold each pastry round in half to enclose the filling. Use a fork to press around the edges to seal; alternatively, pleat into a neat pattern.

7 Place the squash on the lined tray; brush with the remaining olive oil. Sprinkle evenly with the cinnamon; season with salt and pepper to taste. Brush the top of each empanada with a little of the beaten egg; sprinkle with the polenta. Bake on the centre shelf of the oven with the squash on another shelf for 30 minutes or until the empanadas are golden and the squash is tender and browned.

8 Serve the empanadas with lime wedges for squeezing over and chilli sauce for dipping.

Sherry braised beef

DOUBLE BATCH | PREP + COOK TIME **4 HOURS 15 MINUTES** | SERVES **8**

There is nothing secondary about so-called secondary cuts. These not-so-lean cuts are actually the cook's best friend. Not only are they much more forgiving than leaner cuts, but they are cheaper, too. Best of all, they carry far more flavour than leaner prime cuts, which are easily overcooked, and are the perfect choices for braises such as the recipe here.

2 tbsp olive oil

1.7kg piece of beef chuck, excess fat trimmed

1 beef stock cube (10g), dissolved in 2 cups (500ml) boiling water

$^3/_4$ cup (180ml) sweet sherry

1 tbsp finely chopped preserved lemon

40g butter

6 garlic cloves, thinly sliced

375g fresh lasagne sheets, cut into wide strips (see tips)

2 slices of toasted bread, torn

salt and freshly ground black pepper

herbs of choice, to serve

1 Preheat the oven to 160°C (140°C fan/325°F/Gas 3).

2 Heat the olive oil in a 5.75-litre cast-iron or other flameproof casserole over a medium-high heat; cook the beef, turning, for 5 minutes or until browned all over. Add the beef stock, sherry, preserved lemon zest, butter, and garlic; bring to a simmer.

3 Cover the casserole with a lid; transfer to the oven. Cook for $3^3/_4$ hours or until the meat falls apart. Remove the beef from the dish; pull apart into large pieces using 2 forks.

4 Skim any fat from the surface of the cooking liquid in the casserole. Place the casserole on the stove over a low heat; simmer the cooking liquid for 15 minutes or until thickened and reduced by half. Return the beef pieces to the casserole. Season with salt and pepper to taste.

5 Cook the pasta in a large saucepan of boiling salted water for 2 minutes or until just tender; drain. Return to the pan. Add half of the braised beef; stir to combine.

6 Serve the braised beef and pasta mixture topped with the toasted bread and herbs of choice. Transfer the remaining braised beef to an airtight container; allow to cool, then store until needed (see tips).

TIPS

• This quantity of lasagne sheets is enough to accompany the served portion of braised beef. Cook the same amount of lasagne sheets again (or your favourite pasta) while reheating the stored portion.

• Refrigerate the braised beef in an airtight container for up to 3 days. Alternatively, freeze for up to 3 months; thaw in the fridge, then reheat in a microwave.

Roasted chicken 'n' chips

FAMILY FAVOURITE | PREP + COOK TIME **1 HOUR 15 MINUTES + REFRIGERATION** | SERVES **4**

This more wholesome take on the takeaway favourite is delicious and has its own "secret" chicken spice rub. And if you save the chicken carcass and backbone (see tips), you can use them to make soup another day. Add some sliced avocado to the salad, if you like.

1.6kg whole chicken

$1/3$ cup (80ml) olive oil

2 garlic cloves, crushed

2 tsp ground cumin

2 tsp ground coriander

1 tsp smoked paprika

1 tsp cinnamon sugar (see tips)

1 tsp ground turmeric

$1/2$ tsp Mexican chilli powder

100g mixed salad leaves (optional)

1 tbsp lemon juice

200g Greek-style yogurt

salt and freshly ground black pepper

lemon wedges, to serve (optional)

sweet potato chips

500g white sweet potatoes

500g orange sweet potatoes

$1/3$ cup (80ml) olive oil

TIPS

▪ You can also use the spice mix to coat chicken drumsticks or thighs on the bone, then roast for 25 minutes or until cooked through.

▪ Make your own cinnamon sugar using $3/4$ teaspoon sugar and $1/4$ teaspoon ground cinnamon, if you like.

▪ Freeze the unused backbone and stripped carcass for up to 3 months, to make your own chicken stock or use as the base of a soup.

1 Pat the chicken dry with kitchen paper. Place the chicken, breast-side down, on a clean chopping board. Using poultry shears or sharp scissors, cut down either side of the backbone; discard (see tips). Open out the chicken to lie flat. Turn breast-side up; press firmly with the heel of your hand to flatten. Tuck under the wings; place in an ovenproof dish.

2 Combine 2 tablespoons of the olive oil, garlic, and spices in a small bowl; mix well; season with salt and pepper to taste. Reserve 3 teaspoons of the spice mixture; rub the remaining spice mixture all over the chicken. Cover; refrigerate for 1 hour.

3 Preheat the oven to 220°C (200°C fan/425°F/Gas 7).

4 Roast the chicken for 50 minutes or until cooked through and the juices run clear when a knife is inserted into a thigh joint. Cover loosely with foil; allow to stand for 10 minutes.

5 Meanwhile, to make the sweet potato chips, wash and scrub the sweet potatoes; pat dry. Line 2 large baking trays with baking parchment. Cut the sweet potatoes into even 2cm-thick chip-sized pieces. Place on the baking trays in a single layer; drizzle with vegetable oil. Season with salt and pepper to taste. Roast the sweet potato for 20 minutes, turning halfway through the cooking time, or until tender, browned, and crisp.

6 Put the salad leaves in a small bowl. Drizzle with the remaining olive oil and the lemon juice; toss to combine.

7 In a small bowl, gently stir together the yogurt and reserved 3 teaspoons spice mixture to combine.

8 Serve the chicken with the sweet potato chips, salad leaves, spiced yogurt, and lemon wedges for squeezing over, if you like.

Soy and star anise braised pork ribs

DOUBLE BATCH | PREP + COOK TIME **2 HOURS 40 MINUTES** | SERVES **6**

The secret to these tender, juicy ribs is patience and long, slow cooking to break down the connective tissues, while ginger, soy, and chilli combine to add a delicious depth of flavour to the meat. Don't forget to load up on napkins for sticky fingers!

2kg American-style pork rib racks

2 tbsp groundnut oil

1 bunch of coriander (100g)

8 shallots, coarsely chopped

4 garlic cloves, crushed

5cm piece of fresh root ginger, cut into matchsticks

2 long red chillies, seeded, finely chopped

1 cup (250ml) Shaoxing rice wine or dry sherry

1 cup (250ml) soy sauce

1 chicken stock cube (10g), dissolved in 2 cups (500ml) boiling water

½ cup (110g) firmly packed soft brown sugar

3 star anise or 2 cinnamon sticks

200g fresh shiitake mushrooms

steamed rice, to serve

1 Preheat the oven to 160°C (140°C fan/325°F/Gas 3).

2 Cut the pork into pieces that will fit into a 6.75-litre cast-iron or other flameproof casserole. Heat 1 tablespoon of the groundnut oil in the dish. Cook the pork, in batches, for 3 minutes on each side or until browned; transfer each batch to a plate.

3 Remove the leaves from the coriander; refrigerate until needed. Finely chop the roots and stems.

4 Heat the remaining groundnut oil in the same casserole. Add the shallots, garlic, ginger, chilli, and chopped coriander roots and stems; cook, stirring, for 3 minutes or until the shallots soften.

5 Combine the rice wine, soy sauce, chicken stock, and sugar. Add to the casserole, then add the star anise and mushrooms. Return the pork to the dish; bring to the boil. Cover with a tight-fitting lid. Transfer to the oven; bake for 2 hours or until the pork is tender.

6 Serve half of the pork ribs topped with the reserved coriander leaves and accompanied by steamed rice. Transfer the remaining pork ribs to an airtight container; allow to cool, then store until needed (see tip).

TIP

Refrigerate the pork ribs for up to 3 days. Alternatively, freeze for up to 3 months; thaw in the fridge, then reheat in a microwave.

Roast chimichurri chicken with pan stuffing

FAMILY FAVOURITE | PREP + COOK TIME **1 HOUR 30 MINUTES + STANDING** | SERVES **4**

Roasting the stuffing and chicken separately ensures the stuffing is golden and a little crisp, while the chicken is cooked through. Green chimichurri serves a dual role, as flavouring for the stuffing and a fresh salsa. Sprinkle with coriander leaves before serving, if you like.

4 carrots (480g)

4 potatoes (800g), quartered

1.6kg whole chicken

2 tbsp olive oil

140g cured chorizo sausages, coarsely chopped

1 onion (150g), coarsely chopped

4 cups (280g) coarsely torn wholemeal breadcrumbs

¼ cup (10g) finely chopped flat-leaf parsley

1 tbsp currants

1 egg, lightly beaten

salt and freshly ground black pepper

chimichurri

2 cups (50g) firmly packed flat-leaf parsley

1 bunch of coriander (100g), stems and leaves coarsely chopped

2 spring onions, chopped

3 garlic cloves, crushed

2 tbsp olive oil

¼ cup (30g) pickled jalapeño chillies, sliced

¼ cup (60ml) jalapeño pickling liquid

1   To make the chimichurri, process the ingredients until a bright-green paste forms; season with salt to taste. Reserve 2 tablespoons of chimichurri for the stuffing. Set the chimichurri aside.

2   Grate one of the carrots; set aside. Cut the remaining carrots into 4cm lengths; put in a medium saucepan with the potatoes. Cover with cold water and bring to the boil; remove from the heat. Allow to stand for 10 minutes; drain.

3   Preheat the oven to 180°C (160°C fan/350°F/Gas 4). Oil and line a large baking tray with baking parchment.

4   Pat the chicken dry with kitchen paper. Place the chicken, breast-side down, on a clean chopping board. Using poultry shears or sharp scissors, cut down either side of the backbone; discard. Open out the chicken to lie flat. Turn breast-side up and push down to flatten; tuck under the wings. Rub the chicken with 3 tablespoons of the chimichurri; place in a roasting tin. Put the carrots and potatoes in another roasting tin; drizzle with 1 tablespoon of the olive oil, season with salt and pepper.

5   Roast the chicken and vegetables for 15 minutes; spoon the pan juices over the vegetables.

6   Meanwhile, heat the remaining olive oil in a heavy-based frying pan over a high heat. Add the chorizo and onion; cook for 5 minutes until softened and fragrant. Transfer to a bowl; add the breadcrumbs, parsley, currants, grated carrot, egg, and the reserved 2 tablespoons chimichurri. Stir to combine well, transfer to the lined tray; spread evenly. Put on the lower oven shelf. Roast for a further 45 minutes or until the chicken, vegetables, and stuffing are browned and cooked through; stir the stuffing occasionally with a fork to ensure it cooks evenly.

7   Allow the chicken to rest, covered loosely with foil, for 10 minutes. Serve, quartered, with the vegetables, stuffing, and any remaining chimichurri.

Oven-barbecued pork ribs with apple slaw

FAMILY FAVOURITE | PREP + COOK TIME **1 HOUR 30 MINUTES** | SERVES **4**

This oven version of barbecue ribs replicates the flavours very well and is perfect for those without a barbecue or who want to cook 'barbecue' year-round. Also, while spare ribs are not as tender as back ribs, they have more meat on them and are usually less expensive.

1 cup (250ml) barbecue sauce

¼ cup (60ml) Worcestershire sauce

1 tbsp apple cider vinegar

2 tsp smoked paprika

1 tsp garlic salt

½ tsp dried chilli flakes

2.5kg American-style pork spare ribs, cut into 4-rib sections

4 sweetcorn cobs (1kg)

40g butter, softened

salt and freshly ground black pepper

apple slaw

500g green cabbage, thinly sliced

2 apples (300g), cut into julienne

1 large fennel bulb (550g), thinly sliced (see tips)

1 cup (250ml) Creamy Ranch Dressing (see page 148)

½ cup (10g) mint leaves

1 Preheat the oven to 200°C (180°C fan/400°F/Gas 6).

2 Combine the barbecue sauce, Worcestershire sauce, cider vinegar, smoked paprika, garlic salt, and chilli flakes in a small bowl or jug. Place the ribs in a large roasting tin. Pour over the marinade; turn to coat evenly. Cover tightly with foil; roast for 30 minutes.

3 Meanwhile, remove the husks and silks from the sweetcorn, keeping the ends intact, if you like; spread the butter over the sweetcorn. Place on a baking tray, season with salt and pepper to taste.

4 Remove the foil from the ribs; return to the oven with the sweetcorn. Roast, turning once halfway through the cooking time, brushing the ribs all over with the marinade, for a further 25 minutes or until the pork is sticky and the meat is tender. Meanwhile, roast the sweetcorn for the remaining 25 minutes of the pork cooking time or until cooked through.

5 To make the apple slaw, combine the cabbage, apple, fennel, and ranch dressing in a large bowl; season with salt and pepper to taste. Add the mint just before serving; stir gently to combine.

6 Serve the ribs with the apple slaw and sweetcorn.

TIPS

- If time permits, marinate the ribs, covered, for up to 24 hours ahead in the fridge.
- You can swap the fennel for 1 cup (75g) thinly sliced red cabbage and a grated carrot, if you like.

Agrodolce chicken with nut crumble

DOUBLE BATCH | PREP + COOK TIME **2 HOURS** | SERVES **6**

Agrodolce is a Sicilian style of sauce – also found in Calabrian cuisine – with links stretching back to Arab influences on the food of the island and characterized by its balance of sweet and sour flavours. Here, raisins, sugar, and onions provide sweetness, and vinegar sharpness. The nutty crumb topping serves as an inviting textural counterpoint to the pan juices.

2 tbsp olive oil

100g cubetti di pancetta or unsmoked bacon

³/₄ cup (185ml) dry red wine

1 chicken stock cube (10g), dissolved in 2 cups (500ml) water

1 cup (250ml) red wine vinegar

¹/₂ cup (110g) firmly packed soft brown sugar

¹/₂ cup (75g) raisins

2 x 5cm sprigs of rosemary

12 red onions (about 2kg), peeled, tops and roots still attached, halved crossways

12 chicken thighs (2.4kg), any excess fat trimmed

¹/₄ cup (60ml) Dijon mustard

salt and freshly ground black pepper

chopped flat-leaf parsley, to serve

pine nut crumble

8 slices of white bread (360g)

¹/₃ cup (50g) pine nuts

1 cup (20g) flat-leaf parsley leaves, coarsely chopped

¹/₃ cup (25g) grated Parmesan

2 tsp finely grated lemon zest

80g butter, melted

TIP

Refrigerate the agrodolce chicken in an airtight container for up to 2 days. Alternatively, freeze for up to 3 months; thaw in the fridge, then reheat in a microwave.

1 Preheat the oven to 200°C (180°C fan/400°F/Gas 6).

2 Heat 1 tablespoon of the olive oil in a large heavy-based frying pan over a high heat. Cook the pancetta, stirring, for 5 minutes or until crisp. Add the wine; cook for 1 minute or until slightly reduced. Add the chicken stock, vinegar, sugar, raisins, and rosemary; season with salt and pepper to taste. Bring to the boil.

3 Divide the onions, cut-side up, between 2 lightly oiled 4-litre flameproof roasting tins. Pour half of the vinegar mixture over the onions in each tin; wipe the frying pan clean. Transfer the roasting tins to the oven; bake for 20 minutes or until the onions are softened.

4 Meanwhile, to make the pine nut crumble, process the bread until coarsely chopped; season with salt and pepper to taste. Add the remaining ingredients; process until just combined.

5 Heat the remaining olive oil in the cleaned frying pan. Season the chicken with salt and pepper to taste; cook in 2 batches, skin-side down, for 7 minutes or until browned. Place half of the chicken, skin-side up, on top of the onions in each pan. Brush the chicken skin with the Dijon mustard; sprinkle evenly with the pine nut crumble. Bake for a further 40 minutes or until the chicken is cooked through and the nut crumble is golden and crisp.

6 Serve half of the agrodolce chicken topped with the chopped parsley. Transfer the remaining agrodolce chicken to an airtight container; allow to cool, then store until needed (see tip).

Tuna

Salmon mornay pie with celeriac mash

FAMILY FAVOURITE | PREP + COOK TIME **50 MINUTES** | SERVES **4**

Canned fish is an inexpensive way to include some seafood in your diet, and there's no better way to do that than in a family-pleasing pie topped with soft waves of creamy mash. Herbs, lemon, and Parmesan provide a flavour boost, but it all starts with a humble can of salmon.

50g butter

1 onion (150g), thinly sliced

2 garlic cloves, crushed

1/4 cup (35g) plain flour

2 cups (500ml) milk, warmed

150g baby spinach leaves

415g can pink salmon, drained, flaked

2 tbsp coarsely chopped fresh dill, plus extra sprigs, to serve

2 tsp finely grated lemon zest

2 tbsp lemon juice

1/4 cup (20g) finely grated Parmesan

salt and freshly ground black pepper

potato and celeriac mash

400g floury or all-purpose potatoes, coarsely chopped

300g celeriac, coarsely chopped (see tips)

2 tbsp milk

30g butter

1/3 cup (25g) finely grated Parmesan or other cheese of your choice

1 Preheat the oven to 200°C (180°C fan/400°F/Gas 6). Grease a shallow 2-litre (8-cup) ovenproof dish.

2 To make the potato and celeriac mash, boil, steam, or microwave the potato and celeriac, separately, until tender; drain. Mash the potato and celeriac in a large bowl with the milk and butter until smooth. Stir in the Parmesan; season with salt and pepper to taste.

3 Meanwhile, melt the butter in a medium saucepan over a medium-high heat; cook the onion and garlic, stirring, for 5 minutes or until the onion softens. Add the flour; cook, stirring, until the mixture bubbles and thickens. Gradually stir in the milk; cook, stirring, until the mixture boils and thickens. Remove from the heat; stir in the spinach, salmon, dill, lemon zest, and lemon juice. Season with salt and pepper to taste.

4 Spoon the salmon mixture into the prepared dish. Top with the mash, then sprinkle with the Parmesan. Bake for 20 minutes or until the top is golden. Place under a hot grill for 5 minutes or until lightly browned. Serve topped with extra dill.

TIPS

▪ You can swap the celeriac for parsnip or for all potato, if you like.

▪ The recipe can be made in two 1-litre (4-cup) ovenproof dishes as shown in the photograph

Texan-style beef and bean meatloaf

FAMILY FAVOURITE | PREP + COOK TIME **55 MINUTES** | SERVES **4**

The beans in this recipe are a great way of adding more protein and extending the meat. You could also add a finely grated courgette or carrot, if you like; just ensure that you squeeze out excess moisture in the vegetables first. And leftover meatloaf slices with a slice of Swiss cheese make an excellent gourmet sandwich filling for toasting in a sandwich press.

1kg beef mince

400g can red kidney beans, drained, rinsed

35g sachet taco seasoning mix

$^3/_4$ cup (185ml) taco sauce

$^1/_2$ cup (25g) finely chopped coriander leaves and stems

2 eggs

sweet potato wedges and roast tomatoes

2 small orange sweet potatoes (500g), cut into wedges

2 tbsp olive oil

200g cherry vine tomatoes

salt and freshly ground black pepper

1 Preheat the oven to 180°C (160°C fan/350°F/Gas 4). Grease a 25.5cm x 13cm, 8cm deep loaf tin.

2 Mix together the beef mince, kidney beans, taco seasoning, $^1/_2$ cup (125ml) of the taco sauce, coriander, and eggs until well combined. Press into the prepared loaf tin. Pour over the remaining $^1/_4$ cup (60ml) taco sauce. Bake for 45 minutes until lightly golden and cooked through.

3 Meanwhile, to make the sweet potato wedges and roast tomatoes, combine the sweet potatoes and olive oil; season with salt and pepper to taste. Arrange the sweet potatoes on a baking tray lined with baking parchment. Roast for 20 minutes. Add the tomatoes; roast for a further 10 minutes.

4 Serve the meatloaf in slices, accompanied by the sweet potato wedges and roast tomatoes.

PASTA, RICE, NOODLES, AND TORTILLAS

There's a reason staples such as pasta and rice are so popular – they are a fantastic way to build a substantial meal that is not only economical, but ridiculously tasty as well.

Chicken saltimbocca tortelloni

FAMILY FAVOURITE | PREP + COOK TIME **35 MINUTES** | SERVES **4**

Saltimbocca means "jump into the mouth" in Italian, and this quick-to-put-together pasta variation will do just that. To add your own twist to the recipe, choose a different tortelloni, such as spinach and ricotta, or tomato and mozzarella, and swap the sage for basil instead.

8 slices of prosciutto (120g)

340g cheese tortelloni (see tip)

50g butter

1 leek (350g), thinly sliced

200g chestnut mushrooms, sliced

2 garlic cloves, crushed

600g skinless boneless mini chicken breasts, cut into 2.5cm pieces

1/2 cup (125ml) dry white wine

1/2 cup (10g) sage leaves, shredded, plus extra small leaves, to serve

300ml whipping cream

2 courgettes (240g), finely diced

1 lemon (140g)

2 tbsp freshly grated Parmesan

salt and freshly ground black pepper

lemon wedges, to serve

1 Preheat the grill to a high heat. Line a baking tray with baking parchment.

2 Arrange the prosciutto on the lined tray; grill for 1 minute on each side or until crisp. Set aside.

3 Cook the tortelloni in a large saucepan of salted boiling water according to the packet directions until just tender. Drain the pasta; return to the pan to keep warm.

4 Meanwhile, melt the butter in a large, deep frying pan over a medium heat; cook the leek and mushrooms, stirring, for 5 minutes or until softened and lightly browned.

5 Add the garlic and chicken; cook, stirring occasionally, for 3 minutes or until browned. Add the wine; cook for 1 minute or until almost evaporated. Add the sage, cream, and courgettes. Bring to the boil over a high heat, then reduce to a simmer; cook for 2 minutes or until the chicken is cooked through.

6 Using a zesting tool, remove the zest from the lemon in long, thin strips; juice the lemon. Add the chicken mixture and lemon juice to the reserved pasta. Season with salt and pepper to taste; toss to combine.

7 Top the pasta mixture with the torn prosciutto, strips of lemon zest, Parmesan, and extra sage leaves. Serve with the lemon wedges for squeezing over.

TIP

You can use dried tortelloni for this recipe or fresh versions from the refrigerator section. You could also use 500g fresh fettuccine instead, if you like.

Pork larb with broccolini and noodles

EXPRESS DINNER | PREP + COOK TIME **25 MINUTES** | SERVES **4**

Larb, considered a national dish in Laos, has spread in popularity to other parts of Southeast Asia. A fragrant salad made with meat and aromatic herbs, it is traditionally served scooped into lettuce leaves; our version partners with noodles instead for a heartier meal.

1 tbsp groundnut oil

2 garlic cloves, crushed

600g pork mince or chicken mince

1/3 cup (90g) grated palm sugar

2 tbsp fish sauce

4 fresh makrut lime leaves, finely sliced (see tips)

1/2 cup (40g) fried shallots

1/3 cup (45g) roasted unsalted peanuts, plus extra 2 tbsp, coarsely chopped

350g broccolini (Tenderstem broccoli), trimmed, halved lengthways

250g fresh egg noodles

1 tbsp lime juice

1 cup (30g) coriander leaves

1 long red chilli, thinly sliced

2 tbsp coarsely chopped roasted unsalted peanuts

1 Heat the groundnut oil in a wok over a high heat; stir-fry the garlic and pork for 5 minutes or until the pork is browned.

2 Add the palm sugar, fish sauce, makrut lime leaves, shallots, and the 1/3 cup (45g) peanuts to the wok. Reduce the heat to low; stir-fry for 2 minutes or until the mixture is slightly dry and sticky.

3 Meanwhile, boil, steam, or microwave the broccolini; drain well. Cook the noodles according to the packet directions.

4 Remove the larb from the heat; add the lime juice, three-quarters of the coriander, cooked noodles, and broccolini.

5 Serve the larb scattered with the remaining coriander, chilli, and the extra 2 tablespoons chopped peanuts.

TIPS

• Fried shallots are available from Asian grocers and supermarkets. Look for a good-quality brand.
• The makrut lime leaves can be replaced with 1 finely chopped lemongrass stalk or the grated zest of the lime before you juice it for the larb.
• Substitute broccoli for the broccolini, if you like.
• Any leftover larb can be served cold in lettuce leaves for an easy lunch.

Tuna and chilli pasta with dukkah crumbs

EXPRESS DINNER | PREP + COOK TIME **35 MINUTES** | SERVES **4**

The Egyptian blend of spices, herbs, and nuts known as dukkah makes a wonderful condiment for this pasta. Use leftovers on meat, fish, or roast vegetables, or even sprinkled over a salad for texture and flavour. And don't be afraid of the anchovies – they will melt into the other ingredients, and topped with the dukkah breadcrumbs give the pasta a wonderful flavour.

500g dried linguine

2¹/₂ cups (175g) coarsely torn sourdough bread

¹/₂ cup (125ml) olive oil

1 red onion (170g), finely chopped

3 garlic cloves, crushed

2 long red chillies, seeded, finely chopped

8 anchovy fillets in oil, drained, finely chopped

425g can tuna in chilli oil (see tips)

120g baby rocket leaves

2 tbsp dukkah

1 Cook the pasta in a large saucepan of salted boiling water according to the packet directions until just tender. Drain, reserving ¹/₂ cup (125ml) of the cooking liquid. Return the pasta to the pan.

2 Meanwhile, blend or process the bread until coarsely chopped.

3 Heat 2 tablespoons of the olive oil in a medium frying pan over a medium heat; cook the onion, stirring, for 5 minutes or until softened. Add the garlic, chilli, and anchovies; cook, stirring, for 1 minute or until fragrant. Add the chilli mixture to the pasta with the tuna, rocket, and reserved cooking liquid; toss to combine.

4 Heat 2 tablespoons of the remaining olive oil in the same frying pan over a medium heat. Add the breadcrumbs; cook, stirring, for 5 minutes or until golden and crisp. Stir in the dukkah.

5 Serve the pasta mixture sprinkled with the dukkah breadcrumbs and drizzled with the remaining olive oil.

TIPS

- If you prefer a less spicy dish, omit the fresh chilli and use regular canned tuna in oil.
- Serve the pasta sprinkled with chopped toasted pine nuts or pistachios, if you like.
- You could also use a short dried pasta such as penne instead of linguine for this recipe.

Apricot chicken with creamy rice

FAMILY FAVOURITE | PREP + COOK TIME **1 HOUR** | SERVES **4**

Apricot chicken is a retro favourite harking back to the 1970s. While its origins aren't clear, with some suggestions it was created as a way to use up a popular brand of dried soup mix, it has nevertheless remained a stalwart of many a dinner table.

410g can apricot halves in fruit juice

2 tbsp olive oil

12 chicken drumsticks (1.2kg), skin removed

2 large onions (400g), thickly sliced

2 tsp ginger paste

2 garlic cloves, crushed

3 trimmed celery sticks (300g), finely chopped

40g packet French onion soup mix

1 cup (200g) medium-grain rice

30g baby spinach

1 tbsp finely chopped flat-leaf parsley

1 Blend or process the apricots, canning juices, and 1 cup (250ml) water until smooth. Set aside.

2 Heat 1 tablespoon of the olive oil in a large frying pan over a high heat. Cook the chicken, in batches, until browned all over; drain on kitchen paper.

3 Heat the remaining 1 tablespoon vegetable oil in the same pan; cook the onions, ginger paste, garlic, and celery, stirring, for 10 minutes or until the onions and celery are lightly browned.

4 Return the chicken to the pan with the apricot purée and soup mix; bring to the boil. Simmer, covered, for about 10 minutes. Add the rice; simmer, uncovered, stirring occasionally, for 30 minutes or until the rice is tender. Stir in the spinach. Sprinkle with the parsley to serve.

TIP

We used trimmed, skinless chicken drumsticks known in Australia as "lovely legs" for this recipe; they save time by you not having to remove the skin, and the lower bone (the hock) is chopped off, but ordinary chicken drumsticks work just as well.

Mexican pulled beef

DO-AHEAD | PREP + COOK TIME **2 HOURS 35 MINUTES** | SERVES **6**

Pulled beef is a versatile way of transforming a tougher, cheaper cut of steak into a melt-in-the-mouth filling for tortillas. Any leftover beef can be used to make a delicious toasted sandwich with melted cheese or as a filling for baked potatoes.

2 tbsp olive oil

1.2kg piece of beef chuck steak, cut into 7cm chunks

1 onion (150g), coarsely chopped

4 garlic cloves, coarsely chopped

1 tbsp Mexican chilli powder (see tips)

1 tbsp smoked paprika

$^3/_4$ cup (180ml) freshly squeezed orange juice

400g can diced tomatoes

1 beef stock cube (10g), dissolved in 2 cups (500ml) boiling water

12 wholegrain mini tortillas (300g), warmed

2 avocados (500g)

400g mixed cherry tomatoes, halved

250g light soured cream

salt and freshly ground black pepper

coriander sprigs and lime wedges, to serve

1 Heat a flameproof casserole over a high heat. Add 1 tablespoon of the olive oil; cook half of the beef for 2 minutes on each side or until browned. Transfer to a plate. Repeat with the remaining beef. Set aside.

2 Reduce the heat to medium, add the remaining 1 tablespoon olive oil, onion, and garlic; cook for 5 minutes or until softened. Add the chilli powder and smoked paprika; cook for 2 minutes or until fragrant.

3 Add the orange juice, scraping the bottom of the dish; bring to the boil over a high heat. Add the tomatoes, beef stock, and beef, stirring until well combined; bring to the boil. Season with salt and pepper to taste.

4 Cover the dish with a tight-fitting lid; reduce the heat to low. Cook for 1$^1/_2$ hours. Remove the lid; simmer, uncovered, for a further 30 minutes or until the meat is tender enough to shred. Shred the beef in the dish using 2 forks; simmer, stirring, over a high heat for 10 minutes or until the sauce is reduced and thickened.

5 Heat a ridged cast-iron grill pan over a high heat; grill each tortilla, one at a time, until warm and soft. Divide the pulled beef among the tortillas. Top with the avocado, tomatoes, soured cream, and coriander. Serve with lime wedges for squeezing over.

TIPS

- Different brands of chilli powder may differ in flavour and heat levels, so adjust the amount to your liking. For those who like it extra spicy, serve with smoky chipotle Tabasco sauce or similar.
- You can grill the tortillas to soften them, or place on a plate with a damp piece of kitchen paper and microwave for 20-second intervals. Heat a fresh batch of tortillas to go with any leftovers.
- The recipe can be prepared to the end of step 4 up to 3 days ahead; refrigerate in an airtight container. Reheat just before serving. Leftovers can be frozen in an airtight container for up to 3 months.

Spinach and ricotta stuffed pasta shell bake

DO-AHEAD | PREP + COOK TIME **1 HOUR 30 MINUTES + COOLING** | SERVES **4**

This comforting bake can be reworked to include a little meat, if you like. Remove the casings from 500g pork and fennel sausages, and cook them off first until golden. Scatter the sausage over the bake before sprinkling with the cheese.

500g dried conchiglioni (large pasta shells)

olive oil for greasing

500g spinach, stems removed

600g ricotta

2 tbsp finely chopped flat-leaf parsley

1 tbsp finely chopped mint

pinch of ground nutmeg

$2^2/_3$ cups (700g) bottled tomato pasta sauce

$^1/_2$ cup (125ml) vegetable stock

$^1/_3$ cup (25g) finely grated Parmesan

mixed salad, to serve

1 Cook the pasta shells in a large saucepan of boiling water for 3 minutes; drain. Allow to cool for 10 minutes. Transfer to a tray.

2 Meanwhile, preheat the oven to 180°C (160°C fan/350°F/Gas 4). Grease a shallow 2-litre (8-cup) ovenproof dish with a little olive oil.

3 Boil, steam, or microwave the spinach until just wilted; drain. Rinse under cold running water; drain. Squeeze any excess liquid from the spinach, then finely chop.

4 Put the spinach, ricotta, parsley, mint, and nutmeg in a large bowl; stir to combine. Spoon the mixture evenly into the pasta shells.

5 Combine the pasta sauce and stock in a jug; pour into the oiled ovenproof dish. Place the filled pasta shells in the dish; sprinkle with half of the Parmesan. Cover the dish tightly with foil; place on an oven tray.

6 Bake for 50 minutes or until the pasta is tender. Remove the foil; bake for a further 10 minutes or until golden. Allow to cool for 10 minutes. Serve topped with the remaining Parmesan.

TIPS

- This recipe can be made in four 2-cup (500ml) shallow ovenproof dishes. Bake, covered with foil, for 30 minutes or until the pasta is tender. Remove the foil; bake for a further 10 minutes.
- You can make the pasta bake up to 3 hours ahead up to the end of step 5. Cover with foil; refrigerate until ready to bake.
- Sprinkle with micro herbs or small basil leaves before serving, if you like.

Vegetable sides

It's very common to struggle to eat your recommended daily amount of vegetables; there are only so many green salads you can have in a week. Our yummy vegetable sides – with spicy potatoes sneaked in for good measure – offer good options for shaking up weekly meal plans.

Garlicky beans with pine nuts

PREP + COOK TIME **20 MINUTES** | SERVES **4**

Boil, steam, or microwave 200g each of trimmed baby green and yellow beans until just tender; drain. Rinse under cold water to refresh; drain. Transfer to a large bowl. Heat ¼ cup (60ml) olive oil and 1 thinly sliced garlic clove in a small frying pan over a low heat until the garlic just changes colour. Add 2 tablespoons toasted pine nuts; stir until heated through. Serve the garlicky beans topped with the pine nut mixture.

Peas and Parmesan crunch

PREP + COOK TIME **20 MINUTES** | SERVES **4**

Finely grate 80g Parmesan. Line a sandwich press with baking parchment. Spread with half of the Parmesan; cover with a sheet of baking parchment. Close the lid of the press; cook for 1 minute or until golden and crisp. Repeat with the remaining Parmesan. Boil 225g each of sugarsnap peas, snow peas (mangetout), and frozen garden peas, in batches, until just tender. Drain; toss with 1 tablespoon olive oil. Top with the crumbled Parmesan crunch.

Paprika potato wedges

PREP + COOK TIME **45 MINUTES** | SERVES **4**

Place 2 baking trays in the oven; preheat the oven to 240°C (220°C fan/475°F/Gas 9). Cut 1kg floury potatoes into wedges. Put the wedges in a large bowl with 2 tablespoons extra virgin olive oil, 40g melted butter, 2 tablespoons rosemary leaves, and 2 teaspoons smoked paprika, then season with sea salt flakes to taste; toss to coat. Arrange the wedges in a single layer on the hot trays. Roast, turning once, for 35 minutes or until golden and crisp. Season again with salt to taste. Serve topped with ½ cup (40g) finely grated Parmesan, if you like.

Steamed Asian greens with char siu sauce

PREP + COOK TIME **25 MINUTES** | SERVES **4**

Layer 350g trimmed broccolini (Tenderstem broccoli), 150g trimmed snow peas (mangetout), 2 halved baby pak choi, and 1 thinly sliced long red chilli in a large bamboo steamer lined with baking parchment. Steam, covered, over a large wok of simmering water for 5 minutes or until the vegetables are just tender. Combine the vegetables, 1½ tablespoons char siu sauce or hoisin sauce, 1 tablespoon light soy sauce, and 2 teaspoons sesame oil in a large bowl. Heat 1 tablespoon groundnut oil in a small saucepan until hot; pour over the vegetable mixture, then toss to combine. Top with 1 tablespoon toasted sesame seeds and a thinly sliced seeded small red chilli, if you like.

Lamb and mint meatballs with risoni

DO-AHEAD | PREP + COOK TIME **50 MINUTES** | SERVES **4**

A little bit of lamb is made to go a long way in this mouth-watering one-pot dish zinging with tastes of the Mediterranean, but beef and even chicken would work just as well here. The risoni soaks up the tangy tomato broth and helps to keep the meatballs juicy and moist.

500g lamb mince

1 cup (70g) stale breadcrumbs

1/4 cup (15g) chopped fresh mint, plus extra small leaves, to serve

1 egg, lightly beaten

1 onion (150g), grated

2 garlic cloves, crushed

1 lemon (140g), zest finely grated

1/4 cup (60ml) olive oil

1 large aubergine (500g), diced

1 1/2 cups (330g) dried risoni pasta

700g bottled passata

1 1/2 cups (375ml) chicken stock

125g feta, crumbled

salt and freshly ground black pepper

lemon wedges, to serve

1 Combine the lamb, breadcrumbs, the 1/4 cup (15g) chopped mint, egg, onion, garlic, and half of the lemon zest in a medium bowl; season well with salt and pepper. Roll 1/4-cup measures of the mixture into balls.

2 Heat half of the olive oil in a large heavy-based frying pan over a medium heat; cook the meatballs, shaking the pan occasionally, until browned all over. Remove from the pan with a slotted spoon; set aside to keep warm.

3 Heat the remaining oil in the same pan over a medium-high heat; cook the aubergine for 4 minutes or until golden brown.

4 Return the meatballs to the pan with the risoni, passata, and chicken stock; stir to combine. Bring to the boil. Reduce the heat to low; simmer, covered, stirring frequently, for 15 minutes or until the meatballs are cooked through and the risoni is tender.

5 Serve the meatball mixture topped with the feta, remaining lemon zest, and extra mint leaves. Season with salt and pepper to taste, and serve with lemon wedges for squeezing over.

TIPS

- The risoni mixture will thicken on standing; if it's too thick, add a little boiling water to loosen.
- If your family aren't aubergine fans, use 1 coarsely chopped large red pepper instead.
- Uncooked meatballs can be frozen in an airtight container for up to 3 months.

Baked "claypot" chicken with ginger and green onion

FAMILY FAVOURITE | PREP + COOK TIME **45 MINUTES + REFRIGERATION** | SERVES **4**

Claypot chicken is a Cantonese dish of marinated meat and rice, traditionally cooked together in a clay pot over charcoal. It takes a little skill to get the temperature right, but our version, cooked in the oven, takes away a lot of the guesswork. Serve with pan-fried fresh shiitake mushrooms and thinly sliced cucumber, and chilli oil for extra spice, if you like.

500g skinless boneless mini chicken breasts

2 tbsp light soy sauce

2 tbsp Shaoxing rice wine or dry sherry

1 tsp sesame oil

1 tbsp finely chopped fresh root ginger

2 spring onions, thinly sliced

2 garlic cloves, finely chopped

^{1}/$_2$ cup (125ml) chicken stock

1 tbsp vegetable oil

1^1/$_2$ cups (300g) white long-grain rice

^{1}/$_2$ cup (15g) coriander leaves

2 long red chillies, seeded, cut into julienne

ginger–green onion sauce

6cm piece of fresh root ginger, peeled, cut into julienne

4 spring onions, thinly sliced

^{1}/$_3$ cup (80ml) vegetable oil

1^1/$_2$ tsp sesame oil

2 tsp light soy sauce

TIPS

- If you are in a hurry, omit the marinating time.
- Finely grate the ginger in the sauce, if you like.
- The ginger–green onion sauce also works well with steamed or pan-fried fish fillets.

1 Put the chicken in a medium bowl. Add 1 tablespoon of the soy sauce, the rice wine, sesame oil, ginger, spring onions, garlic, and a pinch each of sugar and salt; stir to coat the chicken well. Cover; refrigerate for 30 minutes or for up to 6 hours.

2 Combine the remaining soy sauce and chicken stock in a bowl or jug; set aside.

3 Preheat the oven to 180°C (160°C fan/350°F/Gas 4).

4 Heat the sesame oil in a wide ovenproof saucepan with a tight-fitting lid or a flameproof casserole over a medium-high heat. Add the chicken mixture; cook for 2 minutes on each side. Transfer to a bowl.

5 Wash the rice in cold water until the water runs clear; drain well. Add the rice and 2^1/$_4$ cups (560ml) water to same pan; bring to the boil over a high heat. Reduce the heat to low; cook, covered, for 5 minutes.

6 Place the chicken mixture over the rice. Pour over the chicken stock mixture; bring to the boil. Transfer to the oven; cook, covered, for 15 minutes or until the chicken is cooked through at the thickest part and the rice is tender. Remove from the oven; allow to stand, covered, for 5 minutes.

7 Meanwhile, to make the ginger–green onion sauce, combine the ginger and spring onions in a heatproof bowl. Heat the vegetable oil and sesame oil in a small saucepan over a high heat until it starts smoking. Carefully pour the hot oil over the spring onion mixture; it should sizzle. Stir through the soy sauce; set aside to allow the flavours to develop.

8 Sprinkle the chicken and rice mixture with the coriander and chillies. Spoon over a little of the sauce; serve the remainder alongside.

Cheat's pork and fennel lasagne

DO-AHEAD | PREP + COOK TIME **1 HOUR 30 MINUTES + STANDING** | SERVES **8**

This lasagne takes a few shortcuts to make faster work of the preparation by using sausages, as well as a blended ricotta mixture in lieu of the traditional béchamel sauce – and the result is just as scrumptious.

400g Swiss chard, leaves and stems separated

$2/3$ cup (12g) sage leaves

$1/3$ cup (80ml) olive oil

1kg Italian-style pork and fennel sausages, casings removed

1 large onion (200g), finely chopped

2 garlic cloves, crushed

1 cup (250ml) dry white wine (see tips)

2 x 400g cans diced tomatoes

750g smooth soft ricotta

$3/4$ cup (185ml) double cream

$1^3/4$ cups (180g) finely grated Parmesan

375g fresh lasagne sheets

salt and freshly ground black pepper

1 Preheat the oven to 180°C (160°C fan/350°F/Gas 4). Lightly grease a 3.25-litre (14-cup) ovenproof dish.

2 Finely chop the Swiss chard stems and leaves. Finely chop half of the sage.

3 Heat 2 tablespoons of the olive oil in a large heavy-based saucepan over a high heat. Add the sausages, onion, garlic, chard stems, and chopped sage; cook, breaking up the sausagemeat with a wooden spoon, for 20 minutes or until browned. Add the chard leaves and wine in 2 batches; cook, stirring, for 1 minute. Add the tomatoes; bring to the boil. Cook for 5 minutes. Season with salt and pepper to taste.

4 Whisk together the ricotta, cream, and $1^1/4$ cups (125g) of the Parmesan in a large bowl until smooth; season with salt and pepper to taste. Spread $1/2$ cup of the sausage mixture over the bottom of the prepared dish. Top with a quarter of the lasagne sheets. Spread with half of the remaining sausage mixture. Top with another quarter of the lasagne sheets. Spread with half of the ricotta mixture. Repeat the layering with another quarter of the lasagne sheets, sausage mixture, remaining lasagne sheets, and ricotta mixture, finishing with the ricotta mixture; sprinkle with the remaining Parmesan.

5 Bake for 50 minutes or until the top is golden and the pasta is tender; allow to stand for 15 minutes before serving.

6 Meanwhile, heat the remaining olive oil in a small frying pan over a high heat. Carefully add the remaining sage leaves. Cook for 30 seconds or until crisp; drain on kitchen paper. Sprinkle the crisp-fried sage over the lasagne before serving.

TIPS

- Use $1/2$ chicken stock cube and $1/2$ cup (125ml) boiling water instead of white wine, if you like.
- Using smooth ricotta sold in tubs in the chilled section of supermarkets achieves a smooth, fuss-free creamy topping.
- Omit the crisp sage leaves, if you like.
- Store leftovers in the fridge for up to 3 days. Alternatively, freeze in portion-size airtight containers for up to 3 months.

Creamy beef and mushroom pasta with kale chips

EXPRESS DINNER | PREP + COOK TIME **30 MINUTES** | SERVES **4**

A modern take on beef stroganoff using light soured cream, this pasta is quick to get to the table, making it an appealing option for the end of a long, busy day. If you prefer not to make kale chips, simply stir the kale through the pasta until wilted.

40g dried rigatoni

375g beef stir-fry strips

1/4 cup (35g) plain flour

2 tbsp olive oil

20g butter

1 onion (150g), thinly sliced

2 garlic cloves, crushed

400g button mushrooms, quartered

1/3 cup (80ml) brandy

1 beef stock cube (10g), dissolved in
2 cups (500ml) boiling water

1 cup (240g) light soured cream

1/4 cup finely chopped flat-leaf parsley

1/4 cup (25g) finely grated Parmesan

salt and freshly ground black pepper

kale chips

200g torn curly kale

1 garlic clove, crushed

2 tbsp olive oil

1 To make the kale chips, preheat the oven to 220°C (200°C fan/425°F/ Gas 7). Line 2 large baking trays with baking parchment; divide the kale evenly between the trays. Combine the garlic and olive oil; drizzle half over each tray of kale. Toss well to coat, then spread the kale out in a single layer on each tray. Roast, turning the kale and swapping the trays from top to bottom shelves of the oven halfway through the cooking time, for 8 minutes or until the kale is crisp.

2 Cook the pasta in a large saucepan of salted boiling water according to the packet directions until tender; drain.

3 Meanwhile, coat the beef in the flour; shake off any excess. Heat the olive oil in a large saucepan over a high heat; cook the beef, in batches, until browned. Remove from the pan; cover to keep warm.

4 Melt the butter in the same pan. Cook the onion, garlic, and mushrooms, stirring occasionally, until softened. Add the brandy; cook, stirring, for 30 seconds. Pour in the stock; bring to the boil. Reduce the heat to low; cook for 5 minutes. Add the beef and soured cream; stir until smooth. Remove from the heat; season with salt and pepper to taste. Add the parsley; stir until combined.

5 Serve the pasta topped with the beef mixture, Parmesan, and kale chips.

Rocket and tomato burritos

EXPRESS DINNER | PREP + COOK TIME **30 MINUTES** | SERVES **4**

These burritos made with soft flour tortillas are the perfect answer to the mid-week meal rut.
The filling can also be used to fill crisp taco shells or to top greens in a taco salad, if you like.
Whichever way you choose to serve them, they will go down a treat.

500g lamb mince, or minced beef or pork

35g packet taco seasoning mix

400g can crushed tomatoes

425g Mexican-style bean mix (see tip)

1/2 small white onion (80g), finely chopped

150g yellow or red cherry tomatoes, quartered

1 garlic clove, crushed

1 green chilli, finely chopped

1/3 cup (20g) coarsely chopped coriander

4 x 20cm flour tortillas, warmed

50g baby rocket leaves

3/4 cup (90g) grated Cheddar

salt and freshly ground black pepper

1 Cook the lamb mince in a heated oiled pan over a medium-high heat, stirring, for 5 minutes or until browned. Add the seasoning mix, crushed tomatoes, Mexican-style beans, and 1/4 cup (60ml) water to the pan; bring to the boil, then reduce the heat to low-medium. Simmer, uncovered, for 10 minutes or until the mixture thickens; season with salt and pepper to taste.

2 Combine the onion, cherry tomatoes, garlic, chilli, and coriander in a small bowl.

3 Heat a ridged cast-iron grill pan over a high heat; grill each tortilla briefly until softened. You can also place the tortillas on a plate and cover with a piece of damp kitchen paper, then microwave in 20-second intervals until softened.

4 Divide the filling evenly among the tortillas; top with the rocket, tomato mixture, and Cheddar cheese. Season with salt and pepper to taste. Fold or roll up the tortillas to enclose the filling.

TIP

You can choose the spicy canned beans of your choice or substitute black beans instead if you like.

Loaded veg mac 'n' cheese

FAMILY FAVOURITE | PREP + COOK TIME **45 MINUTES** | SERVES **4**

If you can't resist classic comfort food, you'll love this vegged-up version of the traditional family favourite. Buttermilk makes it extra creamy and enhances the flavour of the cheese. Serve with a leafy green salad to round out the meal.

375g cauliflower, trimmed, cut into large florets

1 tbsp olive oil, plus extra for greasing

250g dried macaroni

1 cup (240g) light soured cream

$1^1/_4$ cups (310ml) buttermilk

$^1/_2$ tsp ground nutmeg

1 cup (120g) frozen garden peas

2 tsp finely grated lemon zest

120g baby spinach leaves

$2^1/_2$ cups (250g) coarsely grated Cheddar or a mixture of Cheddar and mozzarella

$^1/_4$ cup (60g) finely grated Parmesan

$^1/_2$ cup (35g) panko breadcrumbs

1 tbsp thyme leaves, plus extra, to serve (optional)

salt and freshly ground black pepper

1 Preheat the oven to 240°C (220°C fan/475°F/Gas 9). Grease four $2^1/_4$-cup (560ml) ovenproof dishes.

2 Place the cauliflower on a large baking tray. Drizzle with the olive oil, then season with salt and pepper to taste. Toss to coat well. Roast for 15 minutes or until almost tender and browned. Reduce the oven temperature to 220°C (200°C fan/425°F/Gas 7).

3 Meanwhile, cook the pasta in a large saucepan of salted boiling water according to the packet directions until just tender (see tips); drain. Set aside.

4 Heat the soured cream and buttermilk in a large heavy-based saucepan over a low heat. Stir in the nutmeg, garden peas, half of the lemon zest, spinach, and three-quarters of the combined Cheddar and Parmesan; stir until well combined. Season with salt and pepper to taste.

5 Put the breadcrumbs and the 1 tablespoon thyme in a small bowl. Add the remaining combined cheeses and lemon zest; stir to combine.

6 Stir the drained cooked pasta into the hot cheese sauce; spoon evenly into the oiled ovenproof dishes. Press the cauliflower pieces into the pasta mixture. Sprinkle evenly with the breadcrumb mixture.

7 Bake for 20 minutes or until the breadcrumbs are browned and the mixture is heated through. Serve topped with extra thyme, if you like.

TIPS

- You can use a 2.5-litre (10-cup) ovenproof dish instead of individual dishes, if you like.
- Cook the pasta in boiling water for 2 minutes less than recommended on the packet directions, so that it will still be quite firm. The pasta will be perfectly cooked after baking.
- Omit the cauliflower and replace it with roasted pumpkin wedges instead, or stir 2 cups (320g) shredded cooked chicken or drained canned tuna in oil into the pasta mixture before baking.

Meatballs with fennel and Swiss chard

DOUBLE BATCH | PREP + COOK TIME **4 HOURS + REFRIGERATION** | SERVES **8**

Before you think, "Oh, no. Not meatballs again!", these delicious examples have a surprise gooey mozzarella centre. Fennel and Swiss chard are added to the sauce to make a rounded and nutritious meal. The second batch of meatballs can be served the same way as the first with pasta, or try stuffing lengths of fresh baguette for a meatball sub.

1.5kg beef mince (see tips)

1¹/₂ cups (105g) stale breadcrumbs

1³/₄ cups (175g) finely grated Parmesan or other cheese of your choice

2 eggs

1 cup (20g) flat-leaf parsley leaves, finely chopped, plus extra, to serve

1 tbsp finely grated lemon zest

4 garlic cloves, crushed

120g mozzarella, cut into 1cm pieces

¹/₃ cup (80ml) olive oil

2 large onions (400g), finely chopped

1 large fennel bulb (550g), trimmed, thinly sliced

3 x 400g jars passata

1 chicken stock cube (10g), dissolved in 1½ cups (375ml) boiling water

4 large Swiss chard leaves (175g), trimmed, finely shredded

salt and freshly ground black pepper

cooked pasta such as cavatelli or penne, to serve

1 Combine the beef, breadcrumbs, 1¹/₂ cups (150g) of the Parmesan, eggs, chopped parsley, lemon zest, and half of the garlic in a large bowl; season with salt and pepper to taste. Roll rounded tablespoons of the mixture into balls, then press a piece of mozzarella into the centre of each meatball, shaping as you go to completely enclose the cheese. Cover; refrigerate for 20 minutes.

2 Preheat the oven to 180°C (160°C fan/350°F/Gas 4).

3 Heat 2 tablespoons of the olive oil in a large frying pan over a high heat. Add half of the meatballs; cook, shaking the pan occasionally, for 5 minutes or until browned all over. Transfer the meatballs to a 3.5-litre (14-cup) ovenproof dish. Repeat with 1 tablespoon of the olive oil and the remaining meatballs.

4 Wipe out the pan. Heat the remaining olive oil in the same pan over a medium-high heat; cook the onions, fennel, and remaining garlic, stirring, for 5 minutes or until softened. Add the passata, chicken stock, and Swiss chard; stir to combine. Bring to a simmer. Add the passata mixture to the meatballs; stir until combined. Season with salt and pepper to taste.

5 Cover the ovenproof dish tightly with 2 layers of foil; bake for 45 minutes or until the meatballs are cooked and the fennel is tender.

6 Serve half of the meatball mixture on a bed of pasta, topped with the remaining Parmesan and extra parsley. Transfer the remaining meatball mixture to an airtight container; allow to cool, then store until needed (see tips).

TIPS

- It is best to use a beef mince that isn't too lean; otherwise the meatballs will be dry. This also tends to be the least expensive, so that's a boon.
- Refrigerate the meatball mixture in an airtight container for up to 3 days. Alternatively, freeze for up to 3 months; thaw in the fridge, then reheat in a microwave.

Cheat's moo shu pork

EXPRESS DINNER | PREP + COOK TIME **35 MINUTES + REFRIGERATION + COOLING** | SERVES **4**

This dish of Northern Chinese origins, popularized in Chinese American cuisine, is sometimes served in thin flour-and-water pancakes. For a speedier and more accessible option, tortillas are now often used as the wrapper of choice. The dish itself takes its name from the yellow flecks of egg that are a key feature and resemble the blossoms of the osmanthus tree.

You will need to start this recipe at least 3 hours ahead

260g pork leg or loin steaks

1½ tbsp light soy sauce

1 tsp white granulated sugar

1 tsp sesame oil

4 eggs, lightly beaten

4 spring onions, thinly sliced

2 tbsp vegetable oil

1 tbsp ginger paste

2 garlic cloves, finely chopped

1 leek (350g), white part only, thinly sliced

200g fresh shiitake mushrooms, thinly sliced

½ chicken stock cube, crumbled

¼ cup (60ml) hoisin sauce

1 tsp cornflour

8 small white corn tortillas (200g)

1 cucumber (130g), cut into julienne

½ cup (40g) beansprouts

1   Using a meat mallet or rolling pin, pound the pork until 5mm thick. Put the pork, soy sauce, and sugar in a bowl; stir to combine. Cover; refrigerate for 3 hours or overnight.

2   Heat the sesame oil in large non-stick frying pan over a high heat; swirl the pan to coat with the oil. Add the beaten eggs; cook for 4 minutes or until the omelette starts to set around the edge. Sprinkle over half of the spring onions. Use a spatula to gently drag the egg mixture from the centre to the edge of the pan; cook until firm. Slide the omelette onto a chopping board. When cool enough to handle, roll the omelette into a log; cut into 1cm-thick slices.

3   Heat half of the vegetable oil in a wok or large heavy-based frying pan over a high heat. Add the pork to the wok; cook for 2 minutes or until browned and just cooked through. Transfer the pork to a plate.

4   Heat the remaining vegetable oil in the wok over a high heat. Add the ginger, garlic, leek, and remaining spring onions; stir-fry for 2 minutes or until the leek is tender. Add the mushrooms; stir-fry for 2 minutes or until golden and cooked.

5   Thinly slice the pork on the diagonal; return the pork to the wok. Combine the stock cube, ¼ cup (60ml) cold water, hoisin sauce, and cornflour in a small bowl; add to the wok. Stir to combine; cook for 4 minutes or until the sauce boils and coats the pork.

6   Meanwhile, warm the tortillas according to the packet directions.

7   Just before serving, divide the pork mixture among the warm tortillas; top evenly with the omelette, cucumber, and beansprouts.

TIP

Serve topped with sriracha or your favourite chilli sauce and herbs, if you like.

Sicilian spaghetti bake

FAMILY FAVOURITE | PREP + COOK TIME **2 HOURS 30 MINUTES** | SERVES **6**

This timbale made with a meat sauce uses spaghetti rather than the more traditional penne, as we like the way it holds the ingredients together. Perfect for filling up on a cold evening or for a weekend lunch, it is rich, earthy, and very satisfying.

3 large aubergines (1.5kg), cut into 3mm slices

cooking oil spray

1 tbsp olive oil, plus extra for greasing

500g beef mince

1 large onion (200g), finely chopped

2 garlic cloves, crushed

400g can chopped tomatoes

$1/2$ tsp dried oregano

2 tbsp tomato purée

250g dried spaghetti

1 cup (120g) frozen garden peas

$3/4$ cup (90g) coarsely grated Cheddar

1 cup (80g) coarsely grated Parmesan

$1/2$ cup (35g) stale breadcrumbs

finely chopped flat-leaf parsley, to serve (optional)

1   Spray the aubergines well with cooking oil. Cook the aubergines in a single layer, in batches, in a large frying pan over a medium heat until lightly browned on both sides. Transfer to a large plate.

2   Heat the olive oil in the same pan over a high heat; cook the beef, stirring, until browned all over. Add the onion and garlic; cook, stirring, for about 2 minutes. Add the tomatoes, oregano, and tomato purée; bring to the boil. Reduce the heat; simmer, uncovered, for 30 minutes or until the liquid is reduced by half.

3   Meanwhile, cook the pasta in a large saucepan of boiling water until tender; drain.

4   Boil, steam, or microwave the peas until tender; drain.

5   Combine the beef mixture with the spaghetti, peas, Cheddar, and Parmesan.

6   Preheat the oven to 180°C (160°C fan/350°F/Gas 4).

7   Grease a deep 22cm round cake tin with olive oil; sprinkle half of the breadcrumbs evenly over the bottom and side of the tin. Place a large slice of the aubergine in the centre of the tin. Next, arrange overlapping slices of aubergine over the bottom and around the side of the tin. Use spoonfuls of the beef mixture to support the aubergine as you work. Spoon the remaining beef mixture into the centre; press down firmly.

8   Arrange the remaining aubergine slices, overlapping each slice, to cover the top of the filling completely; sprinkle with the remaining breadcrumbs.

9   Bake for 30 minutes or until golden brown. Allow to stand for 5 minutes before turning out onto a serving plate. Serve sprinkled with the finely chopped parsley, if you like.

Baked pasta with ham, blue cheese, and fennel

PREP + COOK TIME **45 MINUTES** | SERVES **4**

Snuggle up and enjoy a big bowl of this deliciously cheesy and creamy baked pasta – the ultimate panacea for cooler winter nights. The zingy acidity of the fresh tomato topping provides a perfect counterpoint to the rich sauce.

375g dried conchiglie (pasta shells)

250g ham, thinly sliced

4 eggs, lightly beaten

300ml pouring cream

$1/2$ cup (125ml) milk

200g soft mild blue cheese, crumbled

2 small fennel bulbs (400g), trimmed, thinly sliced, fennel fronds reserved

$1/4$ cup (20g) finely grated Parmesan

250g cherry tomatoes, halved or quartered

1 tbsp olive oil

salt and freshly ground black pepper

1 Preheat the oven to 200°C (180°C fan/400°F/Gas 6).

2 Cook the pasta in a large saucepan of boiling water according to the packet directions until just tender; drain.

3 Meanwhile, cook the ham in a small frying pan over a medium heat, stirring, for 2 minutes or until browned.

4 Combine the ham and pasta in a large bowl with the eggs, cream, milk, blue cheese, and fennel; season with salt and pepper to taste. Transfer the mixture to a greased 2-litre (8-cup) deep ovenproof dish; sprinkle with the Parmesan.

5 Bake the pasta, uncovered, for 15 minutes or until the pasta is heated through. In a small bowl, toss the tomatoes in the olive oil. Top the pasta with the tomato mixture; sprinkle with $1/4$ cup of the reserved fennel fronds before serving.

TIP

Swap the blue cheese for a milder cheese, if you like. Ricotta, feta, and cream cheese would all work well as substitutes.

Slow-cooked bolognese

DOUBLE BATCH | PREP + COOK TIME **2 HOURS 30 MINUTES** | SERVES **8**

What's better than bolognese? Slow-cooked bolognese of course! The slow, gentle cooking maximizes the flavour of the sauce, with the individual flavours of all the ingredients building and melding over the longer cooking time.

2 tbsp olive oil

2 large onions (400g), finely chopped

3 trimmed celery sticks (300g), finely chopped

3 large carrots (540g), finely chopped

200g prosciutto, finely chopped

3 large garlic cloves, crushed

2kg pork and veal mince (see tips)

$1/2$ cup (140g) tomato purée

2 tsp dried oregano leaves

$1^1/2$ cups (375ml) dry red wine

2 x 700g bottles passata

2 beef stock cubes (20g), crumbled

$1^1/2$ tbsp chopped rosemary

4 sprigs of thyme

100g piece of Parmesan, rind removed and reserved

400g spaghetti

salt and freshly ground black pepper

fresh herbs such as basil, to serve (optional)

1 Heat the olive oil in a large heavy-based saucepan over a high heat; cook the onions, celery, carrots, prosciutto, and garlic, stirring, for 5 minutes or until the onions are soft. Add the mince; cook, stirring to break up any clumps, for 10 minutes or until browned.

2 Stir in the tomato purée and oregano; cook, stirring, for 2 minutes. Add the wine, then bring to the boil; simmer for 6 minutes or until reduced by half. Stir in the passata, stock cubes, 2 cups (500ml) water, rosemary, thyme, and Parmesan rind; bring to the boil. Reduce the heat to low; cook, covered and stirring occasionally, for 2 hours or until the mixture is thickened. Remove the Parmesan rind; discard. Season with salt and pepper to taste.

3 Cook the spaghetti in a large saucepan of boiling water for 8 minutes or until just tender. Drain.

4 Grate the remaining piece of Parmesan. Serve half of the bolognese sauce with the spaghetti, topped with the Parmesan and a sprinkling of fresh herbs, if you like. Transfer the remaining bolognese sauce to an airtight container; allow to cool, then store until needed (see tips).

TIPS

- If you cannot find combined pork and veal mince, buy 1kg of each type. Or use beef mince instead.
- The quantities of Parmesan and spaghetti are enough for the served bolognese sauce. Use the same amounts again when you are reheating the stored portion.
- Refrigerate the bolognese sauce for up to 3 days. Alternatively, freeze for up to 3 months; thaw in the fridge, then reheat in a microwave.

Cheesy chicken and bean sandwich-press burritos

EXPRESS DINNER | PREP + COOK TIME 35 MINUTES | MAKES 6 PORTIONS

You can mix up these protein-rich parcels to include a handful of spinach, or by swapping the kidney beans for black beans or a bean mix and using a grated four-cheese blend. You can even plan ahead, freezing any leftover burritos or making a double batch and storing half.

300g skinless boneless mini chicken breasts

20g burrito spice mix

1 tbsp olive oil

400g can red kidney beans, drained, rinsed

4 spring onions, thinly sliced

12 regular wholegrain tortillas

2 cups (240g) coarsely grated Cheddar

250g red grape or cherry tomatoes, sliced

1 cup (30g) coriander leaves

olive oil cooking spray

1½ cups (420g) Greek-style yogurt

60g sliced pickled jalapeños, coarsely chopped

salt and freshly ground black pepper

1 Combine the chicken and burrito spice mix. Heat the olive oil in a large non-stick frying pan over a medium-high heat. Cook the chicken for 3 minutes on each side until cooked through. Transfer to a plate; shred. Combine the beans, spring onions, and shredded chicken in a large bowl; season with salt and pepper to taste.

2 Heat the tortillas by grilling briefly on a hot ridged cast-iron grill pan or placing on a plate with a damp kitchen paper and microwaving for 20 seconds or until soft. To assemble, lay a tortilla down on a clean work surface; top with 2 tablespoons of the Cheddar. Spread ½ cup chicken mixture on the bottom third of the tortilla. Add 20g tomatoes and 1 tablespoon of the coriander leaves. Roll tightly to enclose the filling, tucking in the ends as you go. Repeat with the remaining tortillas, Cheddar, chicken mixture, and tomatoes, to make 12 burritos in total.

3 Spray the burritos with the olive oil cooking spray; toast in a hot sandwich press for 7 minutes or until golden brown and warmed through.

4 Meanwhile, to make the jalapeño yogurt, combine the yogurt and jalapeños in a small bowl.

5 Serve the hot burritos with the jalapeño yogurt.

TIPS

- A sandwich press or panini press makes short work of toasting these burritos. You can also use a ridged cast-iron grill pan, pressing with a spatula.
- To freeze the burritos, wrap the untoasted burritos individually in foil; place 2 each in resealable plastic bags. Label and freeze.
- To reheat, thaw the burritos in the fridge. Place the burritos in their foil onto a hot sandwich press; toast for 12 minutes until golden and warmed through completely.

Tagliatelle with courgettes and prosciutto

EXPRESS DINNER | PREP + COOK TIME **20 MINUTES** | SERVES **4**

This classic pasta dish, with its handful of ingredients, shows exactly how less can be more. Make it during summer when courgettes are cheaper and plentiful. For a winter version, you could try grated butternut squash instead.

375g dried tagliatelle

$^{1}/_{3}$ cup (80ml) olive oil

100g thinly sliced prosciutto

2 small courgettes (180g), thinly sliced

2 garlic cloves, finely chopped

1 long red chilli, sliced

$^{1}/_{4}$ cup (7g) coarsely chopped flat-leaf parsley

$^{1}/_{2}$ cup (40g) shaved Parmesan

salt and freshly ground black pepper

1 lemon, cut into wedges, to serve

1   Cook the pasta in a large saucepan of boiling salted water according to the packet directions until just tender; drain, reserving ½ cup (125ml) of the cooking liquid. Return the pasta to the pan.

2   Meanwhile, heat 1 tablespoon of the olive oil in a medium frying pan over a high heat; cook the prosciutto in a single layer, in batches, for 30 seconds on each side or until browned. Remove from the pan. Reserve some prosciutto for topping the pasta; crumble the remaining prosciutto.

3   Cook the courgettes in the same frying pan over a low heat, stirring, for 3 minutes or until softened but not coloured. Add the remaining olive oil with the garlic and chilli; cook, stirring, for 1 minute or until fragrant.

4   Add the courgette mixture, including the cooking oil, to the hot pasta together with the crumbled prosciutto, parsley, and enough of the reserved cooking liquid to moisten; toss to combine. Season with salt and pepper to taste.

5   Serve the pasta topped with the Parmesan and reserved prosciutto; accompany with the lemon wedges for squeezing over.

TIP

For a vegetarian alternative, omit the prosciutto and use a vegetarian Parmesan.

VEGETABLES, SALADS, AND EGGS

From summery salads to vegetable-laden
omelettes and fritters, take advantage of
plentiful seasonal produce and fresh staples
to bring maximum flavour to the table.

Warm minestrone pasta salad

FAMILY FAVOURITE | PREP + COOK TIME **45 MINUTES** | SERVES **4**

We have taken the Mediterranean flavours of minestrone and reimagined them in a summery salad that works just as well when you are on the go as it does at home. Simply pack the pesto dressing in a separate container for a portable option.

375g dried fusilli

olive oil cooking spray

2 small courgettes (180g), thinly sliced

400g can borlotti beans, drained, rinsed

135g jar roasted red peppers in oil, thickly sliced

200g baby plum tomatoes, halved lengthways

1 small radicchio (150g), trimmed, shredded

1/2 small red onion (50g), finely chopped

200g bocconcini (mozzarella pearls), torn

1/2 cup (15g) fresh basil leaves

salt and freshly ground black pepper

semi-dried tomato pesto

1/2 cup (75g) drained coarsely chopped semi-dried tomatoes, plus 1/4 cup (60ml) reserved oil

11/2 tbsp pine nuts, toasted

11/2 tbsp grated Parmesan

1 tbsp balsamic vinegar

1 garlic clove, crushed

1 tsp dried oregano

1 tsp dried basil

1   To make the semi-dried tomato pesto, process the semi-dried tomatoes, pine nuts, Parmesan, balsamic vinegar, garlic, oregano, and basil until a chunky paste forms. With the motor operating, add the reserved oil from the semi-dried tomatoes in a steady stream; process until combined (you may need to add a little more olive oil if the pesto is too thick). Season with salt and pepper to taste. Set aside.

2   Cook the pasta in a large saucepan of salted boiling water according to the packet directions until tender. Drain, reserving 1/4 cup (60ml) of the cooking liquid. Return the pasta to the pan. Allow to cool slightly.

3   Meanwhile, heat a ridged cast-iron grill pan over a medium-high heat. Spray the courgettes with the cooking spray; cook for 2 minutes on each side or until tender and grill marks appear.

4   Add the reserved pesto, borlotti beans, red peppers, and courgettes to the pasta; cook, stirring gently, over a medium heat for 3 minutes or until warmed through and well combined. Stir in a little of the reserved pasta water if needed to loosen the sauce; remove from the heat. Add the plum tomatoes, radicchio, onion, and bocconcini; toss gently to combine.

5   Transfer the pasta mixture to a platter; sprinkle with the basil leaves. Season with salt and pepper to taste.

TIPS

- You can use drained sun-dried tomatoes in oil instead of semi-dried tomatoes, if you like.
- The radicchio can be swapped for rocket leaves instead.

Thai-style chicken filled omelettes

EXPRESS DINNER | PREP + COOK TIME **40 MINUTES** | SERVES **4**

Eggs are often overlooked as a dinner or supper option, but they really shouldn't be. They are a great way to add protein and extend a more expensive meat, as in these traditional thin omelettes filled with vegetables and chicken.

8 eggs

1/4 tsp ground white pepper

1/4 cup (60ml) fish sauce

1/4 cup (60ml) groundnut oil

6 spring onions, finely chopped

600g chicken mince

1 bunch of coriander (100g), leaves removed, stems and roots finely chopped

2 garlic cloves, crushed

100g green beans, cut into 5mm pieces

100g snow peas (mangetout), shredded

1 large carrot (180g), shredded

1 tbsp oyster sauce

1 tbsp soy sauce

2 tsp soft brown sugar

1 tsp dried basil

1 Whisk the eggs in a medium bowl with half of the white pepper and half of the fish sauce. Heat a wok over a high heat. Add 2 teaspoons of the groundnut oil and 1 tablespoon of the spring onions; swirl to coat.

2 Add a quarter of the egg mixture, swirling to form a 20cm round. Cook for 1 minute; transfer to a plate. Repeat with another 2 teaspoons groundnut oil, spring onion, and egg three times, to make 4 omelettes in total. Set aside to keep warm.

3 Heat the remaining groundnut oil in the wok. Add the chicken; cook, using a wooden spoon to break up any clumps, for 10 minutes or until browned and cooked through. Add the coriander root and stems, remaining spring onions, garlic, and remaining white pepper to the wok; stir-fry for 30 seconds.

4 Add the garlic, green beans, snow peas, and carrot; stir-fry for 1 minute. Stir through the combined remaining fish sauce, oyster and soy sauces, and soft brown sugar; cook for 2 minutes or until reduced slightly. Stir through the coriander leaves.

5 Divide the chicken mixture evenly among the omelettes; fold up to enclose the filling. Serve immediately.

TIPS

• Swap the chicken for pork, turkey, or beef mince, if you like.

• Instead of making omelettes, you can use the chicken mixture to fill iceberg lettuce cups for a Thai-influenced take on Chinese san choy bao.

• Sprinkle with small sprigs of coriander and some extra finely chopped spring onion before serving, if you like.

Cheesy squash with smoky baked beans

VEGETARIAN OPTION | PREP + COOK TIME **45 MINUTES** | SERVES **4**

Hearty and filling, this comfort dish brings together sweet, tangy, and smoky flavours in a melding designed to assuage the hungriest appetite. Roasting the squash with the skin on ensures the flesh doesn't become mushy, bringing out a caramelized sweetness instead.

700g kabocha squash such as Kent

1/2 cup (125ml) olive oil

1 red onion (170g), cut into wedges

3 x 400g cans mixed beans, drained, rinsed

1 x 400g can chickpeas, drained, rinsed

1/4 cup (50g) canned chipotle chillies in adobo sauce

1 tbsp runny honey

2 tbsp barbecue sauce

1 tsp Dijon mustard

700g bottled passata

3/4 cup (90g) coarsely grated Cheddar (see tips)

1/3 cup (40g) coarsely grated smoked Cheddar (see tips)

6 slices of sourdough bread (300g)

1 large garlic clove, halved

2 tbsp finely chopped flat-leaf parsley

salt and freshly ground black pepper

1 Preheat the oven to 220°C (200°C fan/425°F/Gas 7). Line a baking tray with baking parchment.

2 Cut the squash into 4cm wedges; arrange on the prepared tray. Drizzle with 1 tablespoon of the olive oil. Roast for 30 minutes or until golden and tender.

3 Heat 2 tablespoons of the olive oil in a large ovenproof dish or frying pan over a high heat; cook the onion, stirring occasionally, for 4 minutes or until the onion has slightly softened. Add the mixed beans, chickpeas, chillies in adobo sauce, honey, barbecue sauce, and mustard; cook, stirring occasionally, for 3 minutes or until heated through. Stir in the passata; bring to the boil. Boil for 3 minutes or until slightly thickened; season with salt and pepper to taste.

4 Divide the roast squash between 2 ovenproof dishes (or use 1 large one). Top with the tomato and bean mixture; sprinkle with the cheeses. Bake for 15 minutes or until the cheese is lightly browned.

5 Meanwhile, preheat a ridged cast-iron grill pan over a medium heat. Rub one side of each slice of bread with the garlic halves; drizzle with the remaining olive oil. Cook the bread for 1 minute on each side or until grill marks appear.

6 Sprinkle the parsley over the top of the squash and beans. Serve with the crusty garlic bread.

TIPS

- You can use potatoes or orange sweet potato instead of squash, if you like.
- Chipotle chilli with adobo sauce can be found in most good grocers and delicatessens.
- To keep this recipe vegetarian, make sure you use Cheddar-flavoured vegetarian cheese.

Courgette, carrot, and sweetcorn fritters

FAMILY FAVOURITE | PREP + COOK TIME **25 MINUTES** | SERVES **4**

These gluten-free fritters are a great way to encourage children to eat vegetables. They work well for dinner, but are also easily packed into children's – and adults' – lunch boxes, and are just as nice eaten cold as they are warmed with a little tomato chutney.

2 sweetcorn cobs (800g)

2 small courgettes (180g)

2 carrots (240g), coarsely grated

2 eggs, separated

1 cup (180g) rice flour

2 tbsp vegetable oil

salt and freshly ground black pepper

avocado and coriander salsa

1 avocado (250g), coarsely chopped

2 small tomatoes (180g), coarsely chopped

1 tbsp lemon juice

$\frac{1}{4}$ cup (15g) finely chopped coriander

1 Trim the husks and silks from the sweetcorn. Using a sharp knife, remove the sweetcorn kernels. Cook the sweetcorn in a small saucepan of boiling water until tender; drain. Allow to cool.

2 Coarsely grate the courgettes; squeeze out any excess moisture. Combine the courgettes, carrots, sweetcorn, egg yolks, flour, and $\frac{1}{3}$ cup (80ml) water in a medium bowl; season with salt and pepper to taste.

3 Beat the egg whites in a small bowl with an electric mixer until soft peaks form. Fold the egg whites into the vegetable mixture. Shape the mixture into 12 fritters.

4 Heat the vegetable oil in a large frying pan over a medium heat; cook the fritters, in batches, for 2 minutes on each side or until browned and cooked through.

5 Meanwhile, to make the avocado and coriander salsa, combine the ingredients in a small bowl. Season with salt and pepper to taste.

6 Serve the fritters with the avocado and coriander salsa.

TIP

You will need 1 cup (200g) sweetcorn kernels. If you don't have fresh sweetcorn, you can use drained canned sweetcorn instead.

Salt and pepper tofu with sugarsnap stir-fry

VEGETARIAN | PREP + COOK TIME **40 MINUTES + STANDING** | SERVES **4**

A crunchy, peppery coating transforms the tofu in this recipe, creating a great textural contrast between the crispness of the exterior and the creamy silken interior. Pressing the tofu, then patting it dry helps to remove excess moisture, resulting in firmer, crisper tofu. You can serve this with steamed rice, if you like.

600g medium tofu

3 egg whites

1/3 cup (60g) rice flour

1/3 cup (55g) mixed white and black sesame seeds (see tips)

1 tbsp ground white pepper

2 tsp freshly ground black pepper

2 tsp sea salt flakes

vegetable oil for shallow-frying, plus extra 1 tbsp

2 garlic cloves, crushed

2 tsp ginger paste

1 tsp cornflour

1/3 cup (80ml) soy sauce

200g sugarsnap peas, trimmed

170g asparagus, trimmed, halved

1/2 baby wombok (Chinese leaf) (350g), sliced

1/3 cup (80ml) vegetarian oyster sauce

2 tbsp mirin

radish sprouts, to serve (optional)

1 Line a plate with kitchen paper. Top with the tofu; place another piece of kitchen paper and a plate on top of the tofu (make sure the plate is heavy enough to press down slightly on the tofu). Allow to stand, tilted, for 10 minutes to drain. Cut the tofu into triangles about 2cm thick; pat dry with a fresh piece of kitchen paper.

2 Meanwhile, put the egg whites in a shallow bowl; lightly beat. Combine the rice flour, sesame seeds, white pepper, and sea salt flakes in another shallow bowl.

3 Lightly coat the tofu in the egg white, then coat in the rice flour mixture.

4 Heat enough vegetable oil to reach a depth of 1.5cm in a heavy-based non-stick frying pan over a medium heat. Shallow-fry the tofu, in batches, for 2 minutes on each side or until golden. Drain the tofu on kitchen paper.

5 Heat the extra 1 tablespoon vegetable oil in a wok over a high heat; stir-fry the garlic and ginger paste for 1 minute or until fragrant. Add the combined cornflour and soy sauce to the wok with the remaining ingredients except for the sprouts; stir-fry until the sauce boils and slightly thickens. Remove from the heat.

6 Serve the stir-fry topped with the salt and pepper tofu. Sprinkle with radish sprouts, if you like.

TIPS

- Use all white sesame seeds if you don't have any black sesame seeds.
- For a non-vegetarian option, swap the tofu for 600g sliced and scored squid tubes and use regular oyster sauce instead, if you like.

Balsamic roasted squash and red quinoa salad

VEGETARIAN | PREP + COOK TIME **40 MINUTES** | SERVES **4**

Quinoa is gluten-free and has a delicate, slightly nutty taste and chewy texture; it is available from health food shops and at larger supermarkets. Always rinse well before boiling, and use white quinoa instead of red quinoa, if you like, or a mixture of the two.

1kg kabocha squash such as Kent, cut into thin wedges

1 large red onion (300g), cut into wedges

olive oil cooking spray

$^1/_4$ cup (60ml) balsamic vinegar

$^3/_4$ cup (150g) red quinoa, rinsed, drained

100g mixed salad leaves

200g mixed medley tomatoes, halved

100g ricotta, crumbled

$^1/_2$ cup (10g) mint leaves

salt and freshly ground black pepper

lemon wedges, to serve

1   Preheat the oven to 200°C (180°C fan/400°F/Gas 6). Line a baking tray with baking parchment. Place the squash and onion on the tray; lightly spray with the cooking spray. Season with salt and pepper to taste. Roast for 25 minutes. Drizzle with the balsamic vinegar; roast for a further 10 minutes or until tender.

2   Meanwhile, put the quinoa and 1$^1/_2$ cups (375ml) water in a small saucepan. Bring to the boil; reduce the heat to low. Cook, covered, for 12 minutes or until tender. Drain, rinse under cold water; drain again.

3   Combine the quinoa in a large bowl with the squash mixture, salad leaves, tomatoes, ricotta, and mint. Serve with a squeeze of lemon.

TIP

To make this a portable lunch, make the recipe the day before, but keep the salad leaves separate. Reheat the quinoa mixture at work, then mix through the salad leaves. This salad can also be served cold.

Salad dressings

Commercial dressings bought from supermarkets can be full of added sugars and hidden preservatives. Our dressings are not only delicious, but also easy to whip up (and pretty affordable to boot) – and will take your simple garden salad to the next level.

French dressing

PREP TIME **5 MINUTES** | MAKES **1^1/$_3$ CUPS (330ML)**

Combine ^{1}/$_2$ cup (125ml) white wine vinegar, 2 teaspoons Dijon mustard, and ^{1}/$_2$ teaspoon caster sugar in a small bowl. Gradually add ^{2}/$_3$ cup (170ml) olive oil (or other oil of your choice) in a thin, steady stream, whisking continuously until thickened.

Balsamic and garlic dressing

PREP TIME **5 MINUTES** | MAKES **1^1/$_4$ CUPS (310ML)**

Whisk together 2 tablespoons balsamic vinegar (or red wine vinegar), ^{1}/$_4$ cup (60ml) lemon juice, 1 crushed garlic clove, and ^{3}/$_4$ cup (185ml) olive oil (or other oil of your choice) in a small bowl until combined.

Tahini herb dressing

PREP TIME **5 MINUTES** | MAKES **1 CUP (250ML)**

Combine ^{1}/$_2$ cup (135g) tahini, ^{1}/$_4$ cup (60ml) lemon juice, 1 crushed garlic clove, ^{1}/$_4$ cup (60ml) cold water, 2 tablespoons finely chopped coriander, and 2 tablespoons finely chopped chives (or other herbs of your choice) in a small bowl until emulsified; season with salt and freshly ground black pepper to taste.

Creamy ranch dressing

PREP TIME **5 MINUTES** | MAKES **1^1/$_4$ CUPS (310ML)**

Blend ^{1}/$_2$ cup (125ml) mayonnaise, ^{1}/$_4$ cup (60ml) buttermilk, 1 tablespoon white wine vinegar, 1 finely chopped shallot, 1 crushed garlic clove, 1 tablespoon finely chopped chives, 1 tablespoon flat-leaf parsley, and ^{1}/$_4$ tsp sweet paprika until combined.

Chorizo and potato frittata

PREP + COOK TIME **30 MINUTES** | SERVES **4**

Give your usual potato frittata a gutsy flavour kick by adding chorizo, red peppers, and olives.
Serve warm from the oven with a green salad – or take it on a picnic. This frittata is also a
great way to use up any leftover roasted vegetables you might have on hand (see tips).

1 cured chorizo sausage (170g),
thickly sliced diagonally

500g Desiree potatoes, cut into 3cm cubes

1 tbsp olive oil

8 eggs

1/2 cup (125ml) double cream

2 tbsp finely chopped flat-leaf parsley

1/2 cup (120g) drained char-grilled red peppers, sliced

1/4 cup (40g) pitted black olives

salt and freshly ground black pepper

rocket leaves, to serve

1 Cook the chorizo in an 18cm (base measurement) ovenproof frying pan over a high heat until crisp; remove from the pan. Set aside. Wipe the pan clean with kitchen paper.

2 Meanwhile, boil, steam, or microwave the potatoes for 5 minutes or until just tender; drain.

3 Heat the olive oil in the same pan over a high heat; cook the potatoes, stirring, until golden all over.

4 Meanwhile, whisk together the eggs and cream in a large jug until combined. Stir in the parsley; season with salt and pepper to taste.

5 Preheat the grill to a high heat.

6 Add the chorizo, roasted red peppers, and olives to the pan with the potatoes. Pour the egg mixture over the ingredients; cook over a low heat for 6 minutes or until the bottom and side of the egg is almost set.

7 Place the frittata under the grill for 5 minutes or until just set. Turn the frittata onto a large chopping board; cut into wedges to serve. Top with the rocket leaves, if you like.

TIPS

- If adding leftover roasted vegetables, coarsely chop the vegetables, and add to the pan in step 6, before pouring over the egg mixture.
- Grill the frittata about 15cm below the heat element. If the handle of your pan is not heatproof, wrap it in 2 layers of foil.
- Refrigerate the cooled frittata for up to 2 days.

Mexican chicken salad

FAMILY FAVOURITE | PREP + COOK TIME **40 MINUTES + STANDING** | SERVES **4**

Mixing your own spice mixes is a great way to save money in the long term versus buying a packet of seasoning mix. The Mexican spice mixture in this recipe can used tossed over roast potatoes or as a dry rub for other meats.

500g skinless boneless chicken breasts

1 tbsp sweet paprika

1 tbsp ground cumin

1 tbsp ground coriander

1 tsp dried oregano

1 tsp garlic powder

1 tsp Mexican chilli powder

$^1/_4$ cup (60ml) olive oil

$^1/_2$ cup (100g) white quinoa, rinsed

2 sweetcorn cobs (800g), husks and silks removed

400g canned red kidney beans, drained, rinsed

1 small red onion (100g), thinly sliced

250g mixed cherry tomatoes, halved

1 cup (30g) coriander leaves, coarsely chopped

50g mixed salad leaves

$^1/_4$ cup (60ml) lime juice

1 large avocado (320g)

salt and freshly ground black pepper

lime wedges, to serve

1 Combine the chicken, spices, and 1 tablespoon of the olive oil in a large bowl; toss to coat.

2 Put the quinoa and 1 cup (250ml) water in a small heavy-based saucepan; bring to the boil over a medium-high heat. Reduce the heat to low, then simmer, covered, for 10 minutes. Remove from the heat; allow to stand, covered, for 10 minutes until all the liquid has been absorbed. Fluff the quinoa with a fork; season with salt and pepper to taste.

3 Meanwhile, heat a ridged cast-iron grill pan to a medium-high heat. Cook the chicken for 6 minutes on each side or until cooked through. Allow to stand, covered, for 5 minutes or until ready to use; cut into thick slices.

4 Add the sweetcorn to the grill pan; cook for 10 minutes, turning, until tender and grill marks appear. Cut sections of kernels from the sweetcorn cobs, taking care to keep them intact where possible.

5 Combine the quinoa, sweetcorn, kidney beans, onion, tomatoes, coriander, and salad leaves in a large bowl.

6 Whisk together the lime juice and remaining olive oil in a small jug; season with salt and pepper to taste. Add 2 tablespoons to the quinoa mixture; toss to coat well.

7 Transfer the quinoa mixture to a large platter or bowl; drizzle with the remaining dressing. Cut the avocado into slices, and arrange over the top of the salad. Season with salt and pepper to taste; serve with the chicken and lime wedges for squeezing over.

TIPS

- You can add the spices, olive oil, and chicken to a resealable plastic bag and refrigerate for up to a day.
- For ease and convenience, replace the spices with a packet of taco seasoning mix.
- Serve the salad sprinkled with a few coriander sprigs, if you like.

Bibimbap

FAMILY FAVOURITE | PREP + COOK TIME **50 MINUTES + REFRIGERATION** | SERVES **4**

Bibimbap is a Korean rice bowl comprising stir-fried marinated meat and finely cut
vegetables, and crowned with a soft-yolk fried egg, to be broken and stirred through the rice.

500g rump or sirloin steak, thinly sliced
against the grain

1 tbsp ginger paste

3 garlic cloves, finely chopped

3 spring onions, thinly sliced

2 tbsp mirin

¼ cup (60ml) light soy sauce

1 tbsp sesame oil

1¼ cups (245g) white long-grain rice

¼ cup (60ml) vegetable oil

100g fresh shiitake mushrooms, trimmed (see tips)

4 eggs

1 kohlrabi (500g), cut into julienne (see tips)

2 cups (160g) finely shredded red cabbage

4 baby carrots (80g), thinly sliced (see tips)

1 red pepper (200g), cut into julienne

100g pea shoots or beansprouts or alfalfa sprouts

1 tbsp sesame seeds

soy-sesame sauce

2 tsp sesame oil

2 tsp white sesame seeds, toasted

1 tsp light soy sauce

1 garlic clove, crushed

TIPS

- Use fresh mixed Asian mushrooms instead of all
shiitake mushrooms and daikon radish or shaved
baby radishes instead of kohlrabi, if you like.
- Use a mandolin or V-slicer, if you have one, to thinly
slice the carrots.

1 Put the beef, ginger paste, garlic, spring onions, mirin, soy sauce, and
sesame oil in a medium bowl; stir to combine. Cover; refrigerate for
3 hours or overnight.

2 To make the soy-sesame sauce, combine the ingredients in a small bowl.
Set aside.

3 Rinse the rice under cold running water until the water runs clear; drain.
Put the rice in a medium heavy-based saucepan with 1¾ cups (430ml)
water; bring to the boil. Reduce the heat to low; cook, covered, for
12 minutes or until the rice is tender and the water is absorbed. Allow to
stand, still covered.

4 Meanwhile, heat a wok or large heavy-based frying pan over a high
heat. Add 1 tablespoon of the vegetable oil; stir-fry the mushrooms for
4 minutes or until browned. Transfer to a bowl; stir in half of the
soy-sesame sauce.

5 Drain the beef with a slotted spoon or strainer; reserve the marinade.
Heat a clean wok over a high heat; add another 1 tablespoon of the
vegetable oil. Stir-fry half of the beef for 5 minutes or until browned;
transfer to a heatproof bowl. Repeat with another 2 teaspoons of the
vegetable oil and the remaining beef. Add the reserved marinade and the
remaining soy-sesame sauce to the wok; stir-fry for 1 minute or until the
sauce is reduced. Return the beef to the wok; stir-fry for 1 minute or until
coated in the sauce and warmed through.

6 Heat a non-stick frying pan over a medium-high heat. Add the remaining
vegetable oil; cook the eggs until the whites are firm, edges are crisp,
and the yolks are cooked to your liking.

7 Divide the rice among 4 serving bowls; top evenly with the beef mixture,
vegetables, and fried eggs. Sprinkle with the sesame seeds. Mix the
ingredients together in the bowl before eating.

Barbecued chermoula chicken salad

EXPRESS DINNER | PREP + COOK TIME **25 MINUTES** | SERVES **4**

A chermoula-style marinade and the Middle Eastern salad fattoush are used to lift this chicken salad out of the ordinary and into the irresistible, especially on a hot summer's day.

2 garlic cloves

1 small onion (80g), coarsely chopped

1 small red chilli

1 sprig of coriander, stem and root attached

2 tsp ground cumin

1 tsp smoked paprika

1½ tbsp olive oil

1kg chicken thigh fillets

sea salt flakes and freshly ground black pepper

fattoush

180g marinated feta in oil

2 tbsp pomegranate molasses or balsamic vinegar

2 tbsp lemon juice

1 baby cos lettuce (180g), leaves separated and torn

6 radishes (300g), thinly sliced

1 cucumber (130g), thinly sliced lengthways (see tips)

3 spring onions, sliced

250g cherry tomatoes, halved

½ cup (10g) mint leaves

1½ cups (45g) pitta crisps, crushed (see tips)

½ tsp ground sumac (optional)

1 Blend or process the garlic, onion, chilli, coriander, cumin, paprika, and 3 teaspoons of the olive oil until almost smooth. Transfer the mixture to a large bowl; add the chicken, rubbing the mixture all over the chicken. Season with salt and pepper to taste.

2 Cook the chicken in an oiled ridged cast-iron grill pan over a medium-high heat for 10 minutes or until the chicken is browned on both sides and cooked through.

3 Meanwhile, to make the fattoush, drain and reserve the oil from the feta into a jug or small bowl; you will need ¼ cup (60ml). Whisk together the pomegranate molasses, lemon juice, and reserved feta oil in a large bowl; season with salt and pepper to taste. Add the lettuce, radishes, cucumber, spring onions, tomatoes, and mint; toss gently to combine. Top the fattoush with the crumbled feta and pitta crisps; sprinkle with the sumac, if you like.

4 Thickly slice the chicken; drizzle with the remaining olive oil. Serve with the fattoush.

TIPS

- Use a vegetable peeler to cut the cucumber lengthways into thin ribbons.
- Instead of using pitta crisps, toast 1 large split pitta bread on the grill pan.

Chai-roasted butternut squash soup with whipped paneer toasts

DO-AHEAD/VEGETARIAN | PREP + COOK TIME **50 MINUTES** | SERVES **4**

Chai spices are traditionally steeped in milk for a warming and aromatic drink; here the quintessential spices of the blend are cleverly used to spice a butternut squash soup. To add protein to the meal, we have included a spread made from the Indian cheese paneer.

2kg butternut squash, peeled, coarsely chopped

1 tsp ground cardamom

1/2 tsp cracked black pepper

1/2 tsp ground cinnamon

2 tbsp olive oil

1 onion (150g), coarsely chopped

2 garlic cloves, sliced

1 vegetable stock cube (10g), crumbled

1/3 cup (95g) Greek-style yogurt

salt and freshly ground black pepper

sprigs of coriander, to serve

whipped paneer toasts

12 slices of wholemeal sourdough bread

1/3 cup (80ml) olive oil

200g paneer cheese

1 small garlic clove, crushed

1 tsp lemon juice

1 Preheat the oven to 200°C (180°C fan/400°F/Gas 6). Line 2 large baking trays with baking parchment.

2 Arrange the butternut squash in a single layer on the lined trays; sprinkle with the cardamom, cracked black pepper, and cinnamon. Drizzle with 1 tablespoon of the olive oil; roast for 25 minutes or until tender.

3 Heat the remaining 1 tablespoon olive oil in a large heavy-based saucepan over a medium heat. Cook the onion and garlic, stirring, for 5 minutes or until softened. Add the squash, crumbled stock cube, and 3 cups (750ml) water; bring to the boil. Remove from the heat; allow to cool for 10 minutes.

4 Meanwhile, to make the whipped paneer toasts, heat an oiled ridged cast-iron grill pan over a medium heat. Brush the bread slices with 2 tablespoons of the olive oil; grill for 1 minute on each side or until light grill marks appear. Process the paneer and garlic in a food processor, pulsing until the mixture forms a spreadable consistency. With the motor operating, gradually add the lemon juice, then the remaining olive oil; process until light and fluffy. Spread the whipped paneer onto the toasted bread. Season with salt and pepper to taste.

5 Blend or process the squash mixture, in batches, until smooth. Return the soup to the pan; stir over a medium heat until hot. Season with salt and pepper to taste.

6 Divide the soup among 4 serving bowls. Drizzle with the yogurt; season with salt and pepper to taste. Sprinkle with the coriander; serve warm with the paneer toasts.

TIPS

• Paneer is found at South Asian grocers and in the chilled section of larger supermarkets. You can use feta instead of paneer, if you like.

• Freeze the soup in portion-sized airtight containers for up to 1 month.

Courgette "spaghetti" and baked feta with chickpea croutons

VEGETARIAN | PREP + COOK TIME **55 MINUTES** | SERVES **4**

This recipe showcases how amazing plant-based dishes really are. Courgette takes the place of spaghetti, while canned chickpeas are transformed into moreish crisp croutons – although you can omit the croutons and serve with toasted sourdough instead, if you like.

500g cherry vine tomatoes

1/3 cup (80ml) olive oil

1/4 cup (7g) oregano leaves, plus extra 2 tbsp finely chopped

200g piece of feta, sliced into 4 lengthways

1/4 tsp dried chilli flakes (optional)

5 small courgettes (450g)

3 garlic cloves, thinly sliced

2 tsp finely grated lemon zest

1/4 cup (60ml) lemon juice

2 tbsp finely grated Parmesan

salt and freshly ground black pepper

chickpea croutons

400g can chickpeas, drained, rinsed

1 tbsp olive oil

1 tsp smoked paprika

1/4 cup (40g) smoked almonds, coarsely chopped

1 Preheat the oven to 200°C (180°C fan/400°F/Gas 6). Line 2 baking trays with baking parchment.

2 Place the tomatoes on one of the lined trays. Drizzle with 1 tablespoon of the olive oil; sprinkle with 2 tablespoons of the oregano leaves (reserve the rest), and season with salt and pepper to taste. Roast for 20 minutes or until the skins are blistered.

3 Meanwhile, place the feta on the second tray. Drizzle with 1 tablespoon of the olive oil; sprinkle with the chilli and 2 teaspoons of the oregano. Bake for 12 minutes or until the feta is golden.

4 To make the chickpea croutons, combine the ingredients in a medium bowl. Cook the chickpea mixture in a large heavy-based frying pan over a high heat, stirring, for 14 minutes or until crisp. Allow to cool.

5 Using a julienne peeler or spiralizer (see tips), cut the courgettes into long noodles; place in a large bowl.

6 Heat 1 tablespoon of the olive oil in a small frying pan over a medium heat; cook the garlic for 2 minutes or until lightly golden. Stir in the lemon zest, lemon juice, remaining olive oil, extra 2 tablespoons chopped oregano, and the Parmesan.

7 Add the garlic mixture, roasted tomatoes with any cooking juices, and remaining oregano leaves to the courgettes; toss to combine. Season with salt and pepper to taste. Serve the courgette mixture topped with the feta and chickpea croutons.

TIP

To create courgette noodles, you will need a julienne peeler, which looks like a wide-bladed vegetable peeler with a serrated rather than straight blade. Alternatively, use a spiralizer, a hand-cranked machine designed to cut vegetables into noodles or ribbons. Both are available from kitchenware shops.

SWEET TIMES

For those of us for whom dessert is the
answer, or if you're looking for a little
something to round out your day, this array
of delectable treats may prove irresistible.

Lemon curd layer cake

SPECIAL OCCASION | PREP + COOK TIME **1 HOUR 45 MINUTES + REFRIGERATION + STANDING + COOLING** | SERVES **12**

This stunning celebration cake can be created in stages, if you like. Make the cake
and curd a day ahead, and assemble it close to serving. You can decorate it with unsprayed
edible flowers, if you like, but it's equally stunning with no decoration at all.

250g butter, softened

2 tsp vanilla extract

2 cups (440g) caster sugar

4 eggs, lightly beaten

3 cups (450g) self-raising flour

1/2 cup (125ml) milk

1 cup (80g) desiccated coconut

1 cup (280g) plain yogurt

lemon curd

250g butter, chopped

3 eggs

2 tsp finely grated lemon zest

2/3 cup (160ml) lemon juice, strained

1 1/3 cups (295g) caster sugar

2 tsp cornflour

mascarpone frosting

1 cup (250ml) whipping cream

1/2 cup (80g) icing sugar

2 tsp finely grated lemon zest

200g mascarpone

1 To make the lemon curd, combine the ingredients in a medium saucepan over a medium heat. Cook, whisking continuously, until the mixture boils and thickens. Remove from the heat; transfer to a medium bowl. Cover the surface of the mixture with cling film; refrigerate for at least 4 hours or until chilled and set.

2 Preheat the oven to 180°C (160°C fan/350°F/Gas 4). Grease 2 deep 20cm round cake tins; line the bottoms with baking parchment.

3 Using an electric mixer, beat together the butter, vanilla, and sugar in a large bowl until light and fluffy. On low speed, add the beaten egg, a little at a time, alternating with a spoonful of the sifted flour. Gradually add the milk, then the remaining sifted flour, coconut, and yogurt.

4 Divide the mixture evenly between the prepared cake tins; smooth the surface. Bake the cakes for 50 minutes or until a skewer inserted into the centre comes out clean. Allow the cakes to stand in the tins for 10 minutes before turning out, top-side up, onto wire racks to cool.

5 Meanwhile, to make the mascarpone frosting, beat the cream, sifted icing sugar, and lemon zest in a small bowl using an electric mixer until soft peaks form. Put the mascarpone in a medium bowl, and fold the cream mixture into the mascarpone.

6 Split each cake in half horizontally to make 4 layers. Place the bottom layer on a serving plate and spread with one-third of the lemon curd. Repeat the layering with the remaining cake layers and lemon curd, finishing with the top layer of cake. Spread the mascarpone frosting all over the top and side of the layered cake, using a small palette knife to create swirls and peaks.

TIPS

- The uniced cakes are suitable to freeze for up to 3 months.
- Cut the cake with a hot, dry knife for clean slices.

Baked rice puddings with raspberries

FAMILY FAVOURITE | PREP + COOK TIME **35 MINUTES** | SERVES **4**

Rice puddings are best made with medium-grain rice, as it provides the requisite lusciousness but still holds its shape. As this pudding is so delicious, why not make a double batch and store it in the fridge in an airtight container? Reheat gently in a saucepan.

$^1/_3$ cup (65g) white medium-grain rice

2 cups (500ml) milk

$1^1/_2$ tbsp pure maple syrup or runny honey

$^1/_2$ tsp finely grated lemon zest

2 tsp vanilla extract

$^1/_2$ tsp ground cinnamon

250g fresh raspberries (see tips)

1   Rinse the rice under cold running water until the water runs clear.

2   Put the milk, $^3/_4$ cup (185ml) water, 1 tablespoon maple syrup, lemon zest, and vanilla in a small saucepan; bring to a simmer. Add the rice, stirring to separate the grains; bring to the boil. Reduce the heat to low; cook, stirring occasionally, for 20 minutes or until the rice is tender and the liquid reduces and thickens.

3   Divide the rice mixture among four $^1/_2$-cup (125ml) shallow ovenproof dishes. Top each serving with a quarter of the raspberries; fold gently to mix, taking care not to break up the raspberries further. Drizzle with the remaining maple syrup; sprinkle with the cinnamon.

4   Preheat the oven grill to high; grill the puddings for 3 minutes or until the tops are golden. Serve warm.

TIPS

- Use orange zest instead of lemon zest, and nutmeg instead of cinnamon, if you like.
- If fresh raspberries are not in season, you can use frozen or choose another seasonal fruit

Jaffa self-saucing pudding

FAMILY FAVOURITE | PREP + COOK TIME **45 MINUTES** | SERVES **6**

Self-saucing puddings are one of the miracles of desserts. To make one, you pour what seems like an unusual amount of water over the cake batter and dry ingredients in the dish, then miraculously during cooking the water combines with the dry ingredients to form the sauce and find its way to the bottom of the pudding. Definitely not a dessert designed for leftovers!

1 large orange (300g) (see tips)
1/3 cup (50g) self-raising flour
1/3 cup (55g) wholemeal self-raising flour (see tips)
1/4 cup (30g) Dutch-process cocoa powder
1/4 cup (55g) light soft brown sugar
1/3 cup (80ml) milk
1 egg
1 cup (250ml) boiling water
300g vanilla ice cream, to serve

1 Preheat the oven to 150°C (130°C fan/300°F/Gas 2). Lightly grease a 1-litre (4-cup) ovenproof dish.

2 Finely grate the orange as needed to get 1 tablespoon orange zest; shred the remaining zest into long strips. Set aside. Juice the orange (you will need 1 tablespoon orange juice).

3 Sift the flours and 1 1/2 tablespoons of the cocoa powder into a large bowl. Add 1 1/2 tablespoons of the brown sugar; stir to combine.

4 Whisk together the milk, egg, orange juice, and finely grated orange zest in a medium bowl. Add to the flour mixture; fold until just combined.

5 Spoon the pudding mixture into the prepared dish. Place the dish on a baking tray. Combine the remaining cocoa powder and sugar in a small bowl; sprinkle over the pudding. Carefully pour over the boiling water; bake for 25 minutes or until set.

6 Sprinkle the pudding with the reserved shredded orange zest. Serve with the ice cream.

TIPS

• You will need 1 large orange for this recipe – the larger the better, to get the amount of zest needed.
• If you don't have wholemeal self-raising flour, you can use all regular self-raising flour instead.

Apple pie slice

PREP + COOK TIME **35 MINUTES + COOLING** | SERVES **8**

Is it a pie or is it a traybake? And should you have it as a treat for afternoon tea or warm and topped with ice cream for a simple dessert? Whatever you decide, this apple pie slice is definitely perfect for a picnic and tastes heavenly with whipped cinnamon cream.

6 firm apples (900g), peeled, cored, cut into 1cm pieces

1/4 cup (55g) caster sugar, plus extra 1 tbsp

3/4 cup (120g) sultanas

1 tsp mixed spice

2 tsp finely grated lemon zest

2 sheets of shortcrust pastry

1 tbsp milk

1 Combine the apple, caster sugar, and 1 tablespoon water in a large saucepan; cook, uncovered, stirring occasionally, for 10 minutes or until the apple softens. Remove from the heat; stir in the sultanas, mixed spice, and lemon zest. Allow to cool.

2 Preheat the oven to 200°C (180°C fan/400°F/Gas 6). Grease a 20cm x 30cm shallow cake tin; line the bottom with baking parchment, extending the paper 5cm over the long sides of the tin.

3 Place 1 pastry sheet over the bottom of the tin, trimming to fit. Spread the apple filling over the pastry. Top with the remaining pastry sheet; trim the edges. Brush the top of the pastry with the milk; sprinkle with the extra sugar. Bake for 25 minutes. Allow the slice to stand in the tin for 5 minutes, before cutting into slices.

TIP

For an easy dessert, serve the warm apple pie slice with ice cream or whipped cream, dusted with a little ground nutmeg or cinnamon.

Earl Grey bomboloni

PREP + COOK TIME **1 HOUR + REFRIGERATION + STANDING** | MAKES **25**

These little Italian treats are a great starting point if you are new to making doughnuts. Lemon curd isn't hard to make either, but remember there is a fine line between getting it to the right consistency to coat the spoon thickly and not allowing it to boil.

You will need to start this recipe at least 3 hours ahead

80g unsalted butter

1 cup (250ml) milk

3 tsp (10g) dried yeast

1/4 cup (55g) caster sugar, plus extra 1 cup (220g) for dredging

2 Earl Grey teabags

3 cups (450g) plain flour

1/2 tsp table salt

2 egg yolks

vegetable oil for deep-frying

lemon curd

3/4 cup (165g) caster sugar

1 tbsp finely grated lemon zest

1/2 cup (125ml) lemon juice

4 eggs, lightly beaten

150g cold unsalted butter, chopped

TIPS

• If you'd prefer to skip making the lemon curd, you can buy lemon curd instead, or try the cream filling on page 182.

• Bomboloni are best made close to serving. The lemon curd can be stored in the fridge for up to 1 week, while filled or unfilled bomboloni will keep in an airtight container for up to 2 days.

• The bomboloni can be frozen for up to 1 month.

1 Make the lemon curd. Combine the sugar, lemon zest, lemon juice, and eggs in a medium heatproof bowl; place over a medium saucepan of simmering water. Stir for 5 minutes or until the mixture thickens and thickly coats the back of a spoon. Gradually add the butter, stirring after each addition until smooth. Cover the surface of the curd directly with cling film; allow to cool. Refrigerate for 3 hours or until cold.

2 To make the bomboloni, stir the butter and milk in a small saucepan over a high heat until the butter is melted. Allow to cool to lukewarm.

3 Meanwhile, put the yeast, 1 teaspoon of the 1/4 cup (55g) sugar, and 1/4 cup (60ml) lukewarm water in another small bowl; cover and set aside in a warm place until frothy.

4 Remove the tea from the teabags; process the tea with the flour and remaining sugar until finely ground. Put the mixture into the large bowl of an electric mixer fitted with a dough hook. Add the yeast mixture, table salt, and egg yolks; mix for 5 minutes or until it forms a soft, sticky dough. Cover the bowl with cling film. Allow to stand in a warm place for 1 hour or until the dough has doubled in size.

5 Heat enough oil for deep-frying (be careful not to overfill) in a large saucepan or wok to 150°C/300°F (or until bubbles form around the handle of a wooden spoon when placed in the oil).

6 Meanwhile, turn out the dough onto a floured work surface. Roll out until 2cm thick. Cut out rounds of dough using a floured 4cm pastry cutter. Re-roll the scraps and repeat. Deep-fry the rounds, about 6 at a time, for 1 1/2 minutes on each side or until golden brown and cooked through. Drain on kitchen paper, then immediately toss in the extra sugar.

7 Cut a small slit in each bomboloni. Spoon the curd into a piping bag fitted with a 5mm plain tube; pipe into the centre of each bomboloni. Serve the bomboloni warm or at room temperature.

Impossible pie

PREP + COOK TIME **1 HOUR** | SERVES **8**

The reason this pie is "impossible" is because the ingredients separate into three layers while baking. The heavy flour sinks to the bottom of the dish and pretends it's pastry; the light coconut floats to the top to make a kind of crust or topping; and the egg and milk stay happily in the middle, making a delicious custard.

½ cup (75g) plain flour

1 cup (220g) caster sugar

¾ cup (60g) desiccated coconut

4 eggs

1 tsp vanilla extract

125g butter, melted

½ cup (40g) flaked almonds

2 cups (500ml) milk

1 Preheat the oven to 180°C (160°C fan/350°F/Gas 4). Grease a 24cm deep pie dish.

2 Combine the sifted flour, sugar, coconut, eggs, vanilla, butter, and half of the almonds in a large bowl. Gradually add the milk, stirring, until combined. Pour the mixture into the prepared dish.

3 Bake the pie for 35 minutes. Remove from the oven; sprinkle with the remaining almonds. Bake for a further 15 minutes or until lightly browned and set.

TIP

You could add fresh blueberries to the mixture in step 2, before pouring into the dish.

Rainbow jelly cakes

PREP + COOK TIME **1 HOUR + REFRIGERATION + COOLING** | MAKES **48**

These retro-looking cakes are wonderfully simple to make. A colourful alternative to cupcakes and biscuits, they combine your children's favourite aspects of fluffy cakes and wobbly jelly into one teatime treat. Customize the cakes using other jelly flavours, if you like.

250g unsalted butter, softened

1 cup (220g) caster sugar

1 tsp vanilla bean paste

3 eggs, lightly beaten

2 cups (300g) self-raising flour

½ cup (125ml) milk

pinch of salt

135g packet raspberry jelly cubes

135g packet pineapple jelly cubes

135g packet blueberry jelly cubes

2 cups (160g) desiccated coconut

1 Preheat the oven to 180°C (160°C fan/350°F/Gas 4). Grease four 12-hole (40ml) round-based patty pan tins.

2 Beat the butter, sugar, and vanilla bean paste in a medium bowl with an electric mixer until light and fluffy. On low speed, add the beaten egg, a little at a time, alternating with a spoonful of the sifted flour. Gradually add the milk, then the remaining sifted flour and salt.

3 Spoon 1 tablespoon of the mixture into each of the patty pan holes. Bake for 10 minutes or until firm to the touch and golden brown. Stand the cakes in the tins for 2 minutes before turning out onto wire racks to cool. Repeat with the remaining mixture.

4 Meanwhile, make the three jellies according to the packet directions in 3 separate bowls; refrigerate for 20 minutes or until the jelly is set to the consistency of unbeaten egg whites. Place half of the coconut onto a large plate.

5 Dip each cake into one of the jellies, alternating the colours, then toss in the coconut to coat. Place on a tray lined with baking parchment. Top up with the remaining coconut as needed. Refrigerate for 30 minutes or until set.

TIPS

• Choose any flavours of jelly you prefer, varying the colours for best effect.

• Make these cakes in madeleine tins, if you like, or any other type of tin with a rounded base suitable for tartlets or cupcakes. Be careful not to overfill.

• The undipped cakes are suitable to freeze, while finished cakes will keep in an airtight container for up to 3 days

Rhubarb and strawberry cobbler

PREP + COOK TIME **50 MINUTES** | SERVES **6**

Easy as pie and just as tempting, this cobbler will satisfy your sweet tooth with its soft
scone-like dumpling topping and tart–sweet filling of seasonal fruit. Serve it to your loved
ones with a generous dollop of double cream or a good-quality vanilla ice cream.

2 bunches of rhubarb (900g) or
500g trimmed rhubarb stems

500g strawberries, hulled

2 tsp vanilla extract

$^3/_4$ cup (165g) caster sugar, plus extra 2 tsp

3 tsp cornflour

$^3/_4$ cup (110g) self-raising flour

pinch of table salt

30g cold butter, diced

$^3/_4$ cup (180ml) double cream, plus
extra 1 tbsp for brushing

icing sugar, to dust

1   Preheat the oven to 180°C (160°C fan/350°F/Gas 4).

2   Trim the leaves from the rhubarb; discard. Cut the rhubarb stems into
7cm lengths; you will need 500g. Put the rhubarb, strawberries, vanilla,
the $^3/_4$ cup (165g) caster sugar, and cornflour in a large bowl; toss to
combine. Transfer the mixture to a 15cm x 25cm, 1.75-litre (7-cup)
ovenproof dish. Place the dish on a baking tray.

3   Bake the fruit for 15 minutes or until just tender.

4   Put the flour, extra 2 teaspoons caster sugar, and pinch of salt in a large
bowl. Add the butter to the flour mixture; rub in with your fingertips until
the mixture resembles fine crumbs. Make a well in the centre. Add the
$^3/_4$ cup (180ml) double cream; using a dinner knife, "cut" the cream
through the flour mixture, mixing to a soft dough.

5   Turn out the dough onto a clean work surface. Without overworking
the dough, bring it together into a large, rough round. Divide into
16 even-sized dumplings. (These will be rough in appearance.)

6   Arrange the dumplings on top of the hot rhubarb mixture. Brush with
the extra 1 tablespoon double cream. Bake for 15 minutes or until the
dumplings are cooked through and golden.

7   Serve the cobbler warm, dusted with icing sugar.

TIP

The cobbler is best made on the day of serving.

Lemon buttermilk tart

PREP + COOK TIME **1 HOUR 35 MINUTES + REFRIGERATION + STANDING** | SERVES **10**

Creamy with a hint of tang, this twist on a traditional custard tart is delightfully rich but balanced out nicely by the refreshing tartness of lemons and buttermilk. For a more formal dessert, serve it with any kind of berry (such as raspberry, blueberry, strawberry, blackberry), plain or tossed in a little sugar with a splash of orange-flavoured liqueur, if you like.

^{3}/$_4$ cup (115g) plain flour

^{1}/$_3$ cup (50g) white spelt flour

1 tbsp icing sugar, plus extra 1 tsp

^{1}/$_2$ tsp vanilla bean paste or vanilla extract

125g cold butter, chopped

1 egg, separated

buttermilk filling

^{1}/$_2$ cup (110g) caster sugar

1 tbsp cornflour

1^3/$_4$ cups (430ml) buttermilk

3 tsp finely grated lemon zest

^{1}/$_4$ cup (60ml) lemon juice

3 eggs, lightly beaten

1   Process the flours, the 1 tablespoon icing sugar, vanilla, and butter in a food processor until crumbly. Add the egg yolk and 3 teaspoons chilled water; process until the mixture just comes together in a ball. Knead the pastry dough on a lightly floured surface until smooth. Wrap in cling film. Refrigerate for 1 hour.

2   Grease a 3cm deep, 25cm loose-bottomed tart tin. Roll out the pastry between sheets of baking parchment until 5mm thick and large enough to line the tin. Ease the pastry into the tin, gently press over the bottom and side; trim. Prick the pastry base with a fork. Refrigerate for 1 hour.

3   Preheat the oven to 180°C (160°C fan/350°F/Gas 4).

4   Place the tart tin on a baking tray; line the pastry with baking parchment, then fill with dried beans or uncooked rice. Bake blind for 10 minutes. Remove the paper and beans. Gently brush the bottom and inside edge of the tart shell with egg white; bake for a further 10 minutes or until golden and dry. Allow to cool.

5   To make the buttermilk filling, put all of the ingredients in a large jug. Whisk gently to combine, without creating air bubbles.

6   Pour the buttermilk filling into the tart shell; bake for 25 minutes or until just set but still slightly wobbly in the centre. Allow to cool to room temperature, then refrigerate the tart until chilled.

7   Serve dusted with the extra 1 teaspoon icing sugar.

TIPS

• If you don't have spelt flour on hand, simply use all plain flour instead.

• The pastry can be made a day ahead. The tart is best made on the day of serving.

Monte Carlos

PREP + COOK TIME **45 MINUTES + STANDING + COOLING** | MAKES **22**

Almost an institution in Australia, Monte Carlos are a much-loved coconut-based sandwich biscuit with a jam and cream filling. Perfect for an afternoon pick-me-up with a strong cup of tea, they also make a great treat to slip into a lunch box – or eat at any time of day, really.

185g butter, softened

1 tsp vanilla extract

1/2 cup (110g) firmly packed light soft brown sugar

1 egg

1 1/4 cups (185g) self-raising flour

3/4 cup (110g) plain flour

1/2 cup (40g) desiccated coconut

1/4 cup (80g) raspberry jam

cream filling

60g butter

1/2 tsp vanilla extract

3/4 cup (120g) icing sugar

2 tsp milk

1 Preheat the oven to 180°C (160°C fan/350°F/Gas 4). Grease 2 baking trays; line with baking parchment.

2 Beat together the butter, vanilla, sugar, and egg in a small bowl with an electric mixer until smooth. Transfer the mixture to a large bowl; stir in the sifted flours and coconut, in 2 batches, until combined.

3 Roll level tablespoons of the mixture into oval shapes (you should have 44 ovals); place 2.5cm apart on the prepared trays. Flatten slightly, then rough the surface of each oval with a fork.

4 Bake for 12 minutes or until a biscuit can be pushed gently without breaking. Leave the biscuits on the trays for 5 minutes, before transferring to a wire rack to cool.

5 To make the cream filling, using an electric mixer, beat together the butter, vanilla, and sifted icing sugar in a small bowl until pale and fluffy. Beat in the milk until combined.

6 Sandwich the biscuits with the jam and cream filling.

TIPS

▪ You can use whatever jam you prefer for the filling. For a fun variation, use blackberry or blackcurrant jam and pair these with the peanut-brittle swirl ice cream on page 186.

▪ The sandwiched biscuits will keep, refrigerated, in an airtight container for up to 3 days. Unfilled, the plain biscuits will keep in an airtight container at room temperature for up to 1 week.

Upside-down pear cake

PREP + COOK TIME **1 HOUR 20 MINUTES** | SERVES **8**

Orange-cinnamon syrup adds a further dimension to this moist, fruity pear and ginger upside-down cake – a morning-tea treat that is sweet with a touch of spice, or serve it for dessert with double cream for dolloping over the top.

3 Beurre Bosc pears (630g)

1½ cups (330g) firmly packed light soft brown sugar

1 cup (250ml) olive oil

2 tsp finely grated orange zest (see tip)

2 tsp finely grated fresh root ginger

3 eggs

2½ cups (375g) plain flour

2½ tsp baking powder

½ cup (125ml) milk

orange-cinnamon syrup

⅓ cup (80ml) strained orange juice (see tip)

60g butter

1 cup (220g) firmly packed light soft brown sugar

½ tsp ground cinnamon

1   Preheat the oven to 220°C (200°C fan/425°F/Gas 7). Grease a 24cm round cake tin; line with baking parchment.

2   To make the orange-cinnamon syrup, put the ingredients in a small heavy-based saucepan; bring to the boil. Reduce the heat to medium; simmer for 3 minutes or until slightly thickened. Allow to cool.

3   Peel and core the pears; cut each one into 8 wedges. Arrange the pear wedges in a decorative pattern on the bottom of the lined cake tin; pour the orange-cinnamon syrup over the pears.

4   Beat together the brown sugar, olive oil, orange zest, ginger, and eggs in a large bowl with an electric mixer until combined. Gently fold in the combined sifted flour and baking powder, then the milk. Carefully pour the mixture over the pears in the cake tin.

5   Bake the cake for 10 minutes. Reduce the oven temperature to 180°C (160°C fan/350°F/Gas 4); bake for a further 55 minutes or until a skewer inserted into the centre comes out clean. Allow the cake to cool completely in the tin. Carefully turn out onto a platter.

TIP

You will need 1 medium orange (240g) for the amount of grated zest and juice required. Don't forget: grate the zest before you juice the orange.

Banana tarte Tatin

PREP + COOK TIME **1 HOUR 5 MINUTES + FREEZING + STANDING** | SERVES **8**

This special occasion and spectacular-looking tart is surprisingly easy to make, and although the ice cream will need to be started a day ahead it does not require an ice-cream machine.

You will need to start this recipe a day ahead

2 sheets of puff pastry (330g), partially thawed

³/₄ cup (165g) caster sugar

1 tsp vanilla bean paste or vanilla extract

40g butter

6 small bananas (780g), halved lengthways (see tips)

peanut-brittle swirl ice cream

150g dark chocolate, coarsely chopped

¹/₄ cup (40g) roasted salted peanuts, coarsely chopped

300ml whipping cream

395g can sweetened condensed milk

2 tsp vanilla extract

250g mascarpone or vanilla custard

²/₃ cup (185g) crunchy peanut butter (see tips)

TIPS

- Use roasted almonds and almond spread instead of peanuts and peanut butter in the ice cream, if you like.
- We used slightly under-ripe bananas here, as they hold their shape better.

1   To make the peanut brittle, place a 26cm x 13cm loaf tin in the freezer for at least 15 minutes. Line a tray with baking parchment. Melt the chocolate in the microwave on HIGH in 30-seconds bursts, stirring after each burst, until melted. Fold through the peanuts; spread over the baking parchment. Freeze for 10 minutes or until hard. Cut into bite-sized chunks; keep cold. Beat the cream, condensed milk, and vanilla in a large bowl with an electric mixer fitted with a whisk attachment on high speed for 5 minutes or until firm peaks form. Add the mascarpone; beat for another 1 minute or until fluffy again. Fold through the peanut brittle. Spread half the mascarpone mixture into the chilled loaf tin. Use a small spoon to spread half of the peanut butter over the ice-cream mixture. Repeat with remaining ice-cream mixture and peanut butter. Smooth the surface, cover with plastic film; freeze for at least 6 hours or overnight.

2   Preheat the oven to 200°C (180°C fan/400°F/Gas 6).

3   Place one of the pastry sheets directly over the other on a piece of baking parchment. Press with a rolling pin to stick together; roll to about 27cm square. Roughly trim to a 27cm round. Refrigerate until needed.

4   Scatter the sugar over the bottom of a 26cm ovenproof frying pan. Cook over a medium heat for 6 minutes or until the sugar starts to dissolve and caramelize around the edge; continue swirling the pan occasionally until the sugar dissolves and is caramelized (take care that it doesn't burn). Add the vanilla and butter; whisk carefully until combined and emulsified. Remove the pan from the heat; place the banana halves, cut-side down and side by side, over the caramel.

5   Cover the bananas with the pastry; quickly tuck any edges into the side of the pan with a wooden spoon. Using a sharp knife, make 3 small vent holes in the top. Bake for 30 minutes until dark golden and puffed.

6   Allow the tart to stand in the pan for 2 minutes. Place a large plate on top, then shake to loosen the tart from the pan. Working quickly and very carefully, invert the tart onto a plate. Serve hot with the ice cream.

Conversion chart

A note on Australian measures

• One Australian metric measuring cup holds approximately 250ml.

• One Australian metric tablespoon holds 20ml.

• One Australian metric teaspoon holds 5ml.

• The difference between one country's measuring cups and another's is within a two- or three-teaspoon variance, and should not affect your cooking results.

• North America, New Zealand, and the United Kingdom use a 15ml tablespoon.

Using measures in this book

• All cup and spoon measurements are level.

• The most accurate way of measuring dry ingredients is to weigh them.

• When measuring liquids, use a clear glass or plastic jug with metric markings.

• We use large eggs with an average weight of 60g. All fruit and vegetables are assumed to be medium unless otherwise stated.

Dry measures

metric	imperial
15g	$1/2$oz
30g	1oz
60g	2oz
90g	3oz
125g	4oz ($1/4$lb)
155g	5oz
185g	6oz
220g	7oz
250g	8oz ($1/2$lb)
280g	9oz
315g	10oz
345g	11oz
375g	12oz ($3/4$lb)
410g	13oz
440g	14oz
470g	15oz
500g	16oz (1lb)
750g	24oz ($1^{1}/2$lb)
1kg	32oz (2lb)

Liquid measures

metric	imperial
30ml	1 fluid oz
60ml	2 fluid oz
100ml	3 fluid oz
125ml	4 fluid oz
150ml	5 fluid oz
190ml	6 fluid oz
250ml	8 fluid oz
300ml	10 fluid oz
500ml	16 fluid oz
600ml	20 fluid oz
1000ml (1 litre)	$1^{3}/4$ pints

Length measures

metric	imperial
3mm	$1/8$in
6mm	$1/4$in
1cm	$1/2$in
2cm	$3/4$in
2.5cm	1in
5cm	2in
6cm	$2^{1}/2$in
8cm	3in
10cm	4in
13cm	5in
15cm	6in
18cm	7in
20cm	8in
22cm	9in
25cm	10in
28cm	11in
30cm	12in (1ft)

Oven temperatures

The oven temperatures in this book are for conventional ovens; if you have a fan-forced oven, decrease the temperature by 10–20 degrees.

	°C (Celsius)	°F (Fahrenheit)
Very slow	120	250
Slow	150	300
Moderately slow	160	325
Moderate	180	350
Moderately hot	200	400
Hot	220	425
Very hot	240	475

Index

Acknowledgments

DK would like to thank Sophia Young, Joe Reville,
Amanda Chebatte, and Georgia Moore for their
assistance in making this book.

The Australian Women's Weekly Test Kitchen in
Sydney has developed, tested, and photographed
the recipes in this book.